OECD

REVIEWS OF NATIONAL POLICIES FOR EDUCATION

EDUCATIONAL REFORMS IN
SWEDEN

ORGANISATION FOR ECONOMIC CO-OPERATION AND DEVELOPMENT
PARIS 1981

The Organisation for Economic Co-operation and Development (OECD) was set up under a Convention signed in Paris on 14th December 1960, which provides that the OECD shall promote policies designed:
- to achieve the highest sustainable economic growth and employment and a rising standard of living in Member countries, while maintaining financial stability, and thus to contribute to the development of the world economy;
- to contribute to sound economic expansion in Member as well as non-member countries in the process of economic development;
- to contribute to the expansion of world trade on a multilateral, non-discriminatory basis in accordance with international obligations.

The Members of OECD are Australia, Austria, Belgium, Canada, Denmark, Finland, France, the Federal Republic of Germany, Greece, Iceland, Ireland, Italy, Japan, Luxembourg, the Netherlands, New Zealand, Norway, Portugal, Spain, Sweden, Switzerland, Turkey, the United Kingdom and the United States.

Publié en français sous le titre :

**LES RÉFORMES DE L'ENSEIGNEMENT
EN
SUÈDE**

*
* *

© OECD, 1981
Queries concerning permissions or translation rights should be addressed to:
Director of Information, OECD
2, rue André-Pascal, 75775 PARIS CEDEX 16, France.

CONTENTS

Preface 7

The OECD Examiners and the Members of the Swedish Delegation . 9

Part One

THE EXAMINERS' REPORT

I. INTRODUCTION 13

   1. The Importance of the Swedish Example 13
   2. Purposes and Methods of the Review 14

II. A SOCIETY ATTEMPTS TO REFORM ITS EDUCATION 17

   1. The Main Achievements 17
   2. Conformity and Consensus 19
   3. The Dilemmas of Social Reform 20
   4. The Stages of Reform 21
   5. Our Main Themes 23

III. THE DRIVE TOWARDS EQUALITY 25

   1. Increasing Access 25
   2. Social Differentiations Remain 27
   3. Sex Differentiation 28
   4. Regional Disparities 28
   5. The Education of Immigrants 29
   6. Access to Higher Education 31
   7. Admission Rules 31
   8. Adult and Recurrent Education 35
   9. Pre-School Education 37
   10. The Handicapped 38
   11. Some General Points about the Drive Towards Equality . 38

IV. EDUCATION FOR DEMOCRACY AND WORKING LIFE 41

   1. Democratisation of Education 42
   2. The Vocational Content of the Curriculum as
      Prescribed 44
   3. Education for the Labour Market 45

V. STRUCTURE, CONTENT AND METHODS 48

    1. Challenge to Traditional Curricula 48
    2. ... And to Ways of Working 49
    3. Levels of Achievement 50
    4. Modes of Change 51
    5. The Role of Teachers, Education and In-Service Training 52
    6. Units of Action and Development 53
    7. The 1979 Bill 54
    8. The Grading Issue 54
    9. The Gymnasium 55
   10. R & D and In-Service Training 57
   11. Higher Education and Research 59

VI. SOCIAL CHANGE AND POLICY-MAKING 62

    1. Rationality Rather than Ambiguity 62
    2. The Central Institutions 62
    3. Rolling Reform and the Commissions 64
    4. Decentralisation 65
    5. Teacher and Parent Power 67
    6. Higher Education Governance 68
    7. The Regional Boards 69
    8. Student Criticisms 70
    9. Changing the Role of the Centre 72

VII. CONCLUSION 75

    1. Education and its Social Functions 75
    2. The Issue of Equality 76
    3. Educational Content and Methods 77
    4. The School and its Relationship to Parents and the Community 77
    5. Links with Working Life 78
    6. Central Government and Rolling Reform 79
    7. Higher Education 80

Part Two

RECORD OF THE REVIEW MEETING
(Paris, 13th November 1979)

I. EDUCATION AND ITS SOCIAL FUNCTION AND THE ISSUE OF EQUALITY 85

   Upper Secondary Education 87
   Admission to Higher Education 88
   Pre-School Education and Help to the Disadvantaged 89

II.	EDUCATIONAL CONTENT AND METHODS	93
III.	THE SCHOOL AND ITS RELATIONSHIP TO PARENTS AND THE COMMUNITY	96
IV.	HIGHER EDUCATION	97
V.	CENTRAL GOVERNMENT AND ROLLING REFORM	99
VI.	LINKS WITH WORKING LIFE	100
VII.	CONCLUDING REMARKS	101

Annex

    LIST OF MAIN SOURCES CONSULTED 103

PREFACE

In 1967 the OECD completed its first major review of Swedish education at a time when educational expansion was in full swing and when Sweden had already acquired its deserved reputation of being the pioneer in the national planning of education towards egalitarian ends. That review aroused a great deal of interest because of the broad sweep of Sweden's educational reforms and the meticulous planning of administrative structures and monitoring of processes that went into their implementation.

The OECD has now completed a second review in Sweden, against a background different from that obtaining in 1967. While still fully committed to providing a comprehensive and egalitarian education service, Sweden today, like other OECD countries, has become more aware of the complexity and uncertainty that surround all education reform. For this reason the team of OECD Examiners set out purposefully not only to identify the successes of Swedish educational reforms, but also to see where problems lay so that they might give pointers to other educational policy makers as they, too, grapple with uncertainty.

The Examiners derived their arguments and judgements from three sources. First, a substantial background report on compulsory schooling and higher education prepared for their guidance by the Swedish authorities, which has been published by the OECD under the title Goals for Educational Policy in Sweden. This records changes and developments since 1967 and evokes major themes and issues that should attract the attention of the whole international community with a responsibility for education. The second source was a number of published and unpublished documents, both official and unofficial, relating to Swedish education and to pertinent aspects of overall social and economic policy. The third was evidence and impressions gleaned from a two-week tour of the country.

At the customary review meeting held in Paris in November 1979, a Swedish official Delegation answered key questions arising from the Examiners' Report. While admitting the need to tackle the several problems raised, the delegates stressed that some solutions had already been found or were about to be tested. They accepted the hint that there was a certain confusion and lack of morale surrounding the impact of major educational reforms, but argued that there must always be a lag between ambitions and their fulfillment and this they were conscientiously trying to overcome.

The Examiners' Report and the record of the review meeting with the Education Committee are contained in the present volume.

THE OECD EXAMINERS

Professor J.A. van Kemenade (Chairman)	Member of Parliament, (formerly Minister of Education and Science) The Netherlands.
Professor M. Kogan	Brunel University, United Kingdom.
Professor P.G. von Beckerath	Chief Personnel Manager, Bayer A-G Leverkusen, Germany.
Dr. Ingrid Eide	University of Oslo, (formerly Under-Secretary of State, Ministry of Education) Norway.

MEMBERS OF THE SWEDISH DELEGATION

Mr. Anders Arfwedson	Under-Secretary of State, Ministry of Education
Mr. Lars Ekholm	Deputy Head of Department, Ministry of Education
Mr. Erland Ringborg	Deputy Head, The Office of the Chancellor of the Swedish Universities
Mr. Sven-Åke Johansson	Director, Ministry of Education
Mr. Lennart Orehag	Deputy Director-General, the National Board of Education
Ms. Gunilla Hjort	Head of Section, Ministry of Education

Part One

THE EXAMINERS' REPORT

I

INTRODUCTION

In October 1977 the Swedish government invited the OECD to review its education system so as to "enable Sweden to analyse its past, present and proposed education policies and to shed some light on particular aspects of the Swedish system which might be of special interest to an international audience". Our report attempts to meet that request.

1. THE IMPORTANCE OF THE SWEDISH EXAMPLE

We visited Sweden some twelve years after the completion of the first major OECD examination of Swedish education. The change and development since that time, recorded in the Swedish government's Background Report on Compulsory School and Higher Education (1) prepared in February 1979 and to which the reader's attention is directed for detailed discussion of many of the issues covered here, evoke themes and generalisations which should attract the attention of the whole international community with a concern for education. At different times in history, it has fallen to different countries to take a lead which others follow. In the post-war period, and particularly from the mid-1950s to the present, Sweden has been a pioneer of educational reform. Whilst remaining a country of great and self-sustaining traditions, Sweden has been in the forefront of radical social reform in an area of human activity where what is decided affects almost all individuals in the formative years, and every family who invest hope and care in the future of their children.

In Sweden, a small population sustains a highly productive and civilised society. Endowed though the country is with beautiful lakes and forests, it is the Swedes themselves who have created a society that is innately civilised, as exemplified by such lovely cities as Stockholm and Uppsala and by its rich folk culture. Swedes are among the world's leaders in standards of public and domestic design and their innate taste and flair are seen in lavishly equipped and taste-

---
1) <u>Educational Policy and Planning: Goals for Educational Policy in Sweden</u>, OECD, Paris, 1980.

fully created schools. Their contribution to the arts, literary and visual, from Strindberg to Bergman, can be put alongside their exigent standards of technical reliability in engineering. Increasingly, they have deliberately and painstakingly cared for their old and their sick. None of this has come easily. A small population in a long and wide country must maintain thousands of kilometers of road and rail in freezing winters. The geographical characteristics of the country have, indeed, affected its political structure. To have so scattered a population over so wide a territory does not invite easy communication, and creating consensus has been a serious and difficult matter. In the past, the divisions to be found everywhere of age, sex, class, between the urban and the rural and the centre and the periphery accounted for the strong efforts that have gone into the means by which consensus is created, maintained and changed.

At the same time, however, as Swedish life and society seem to express so much that is adventurous and good in human endeavour, Swedes are formal in procedure and social ritual. They are masters, and the servants, of due process. It is perhaps this concern with appropriateness of style, with the need to be considerate and right – even perfect and correct – that makes it difficult for the massive social changes that are thought through so carefully to be implemented at the individual and human level. We shall return to that complex problem of style and impact later in the report.

These historical and human characteristics are well reflected in the education system which has so rapidly changed over the last twenty years. The role of Sweden as an exemplar of civilised standards was indeed impressed on us in the course of our visit as privileged guests for the purpose of our examination. Everywhere we met with hospitality that derived both from pride with what had been achieved and from a concern that what was demonstrated should be fully discussed and analysed. Their hospitality included a determination to share ideas and to extend mutual understanding. Our gratitude to the Swedish government and the scores of people within the Ministry of Education, the National Board of Education, the National Board of Universities and Colleges, and the many other groups in regional boards for higher education, universities and colleges, gymnasia and schools, the Riksdag,(1) trade union and employers' federations, students' and parents' associations, cannot be overstated.

2. PURPOSES AND METHODS OF THE REVIEW

Although the review is intended to consider the formal education system in its entirety, we were asked to concentrate particularly on

---

1) Parliament.

the period of compulsory schooling, that is, grades 1 to 9, which provide education from 7 to 16 years, and higher education as provided in the universities and colleges. We discussed, but in no great detail, upper secondary education which is provided in the gymnasium, in lines of between two and four years from the ages of 16 onwards, but a national commission is currently enquiring into the options for reform and our hosts felt we might thus lighten our load.

Our terms of reference were nonetheless extremely wide and we had no more than two weeks in which to complete intensive visits and discussions. We were greatly assisted by the comprehensive, objective and self-critical analysis contained in the Background Report, "Goals for Educational Policy in Sweden", and by a mass of supplementary papers provided by education authorities and groups at all levels of our enquiry. We had many discussions with a wide range of officials representing the main authorities at the national and local level. We also benefited from visits to universities, colleges, vocational centres and Labour Market Training Centres,(1) gymnasia, schools and pre-school centres. Given, however, the brevity and selectiveness of our visits and the necessarily selective nature of our reading, it will be clear that our examination cannot contain an authoritative evaluation of the quality of education being offered in Sweden. We have to draw attention to evaluations made by others. Nor can we fully analyse the organisational and pedagogical aspects of what is provided in the universities, colleges and schools.

We are concerned rather with testing and internal logic of the organisational structures and the educational assumptions as they are presented to us. Yet, even with such modest objectives, examiners face all but overwhelming problems in evaluating a total education system. Within Sweden itself, and within a very few years, the operating values and the circumstances change. For changes in both consider, for example, the shifts in student demand for - and social expectations of - higher education at the time when the present reforms were being planned (1968) as compared with current assumptions now that they are being fully implemented. Nor are objectives simple and unanimously adopted. At any one time, a statement of intention made by one group is, and perhaps should be, capable of contradiction by another group. Public policies may be developed by exhaustive work within commissions and tested through a period of public debate. There is then, however, a lead-time between the statement of aims and their implementation which differs, moreover, not only in the intentions of those who introduce policies, but also in the willingness and ability of those who implement them. Statements of objectives always hope to be statements of outputs. But national authorities seeking to reform a system are more able to prescribe the input variables than the outcomes. In education, as in all social policy

1) See page 36.

areas, a movement at one stage is often paid for in unpredictable fashion in the next stage. For example, if the compulsory school is made free of grades and of restrictive mechanisms for selecting options, the task of selection by and of pupils may simply be lifted into the next stage. Freedom of choice and of style may be paid for later on if rigour and selection must then be imposed.

No move escapes its unintended consequences. All of the leading concepts which we encounter in Swedish education as elsewhere, such as those of equality, of participation, of efficiency, of quality and of progress, are ambiguous. We will come to the nature of the ambiguities in the main body of our report, but outsiders who evaluate must first clarify the multiple nature of what is to be evaluated.

Because Sweden has invested so much care, resources and hope into reforming its education, ambiguity and uncertainty are all the more obvious. Intentions have been clear and actions deliberate. The examiners did not find it easy to evaluate the results, because they shared with their Swedish hosts the complexity and uncertainty that surround all education reform. We hope that our report will show how the Swedish example gives pointers to other educational policy-makers as they, too, grapple with uncertainty.

II

A SOCIETY ATTEMPTS TO REFORM ITS EDUCATION

1. THE MAIN ACHIEVEMENTS

By many of the criteria which can be applied to a society, Sweden represents a story of success. In the economy, an expansionary policy until 1976 maintained high levels of domestic demand and activity.(1) There were then inflationary pressures, an erosion of competitiveness and growing current external deficit. But prior to the external shock of the second oil crisis, it proved possible to reverse these trends through the devaluation of the Swedish Krona in 1977 and moderate wage and salary settlements negotiated by the central labour and employers' organisations in the spring of 1978. The current external deficit was significantly reduced. By the end of 1978 the rate of inflation had fallen to well below the OECD average. Unemployment remained low and less than 2 per cent were out of work in November 1978. The number of employers engaged in labour market support schemes has increased. It is true that recent legislation – confirming an already developed practice – requires job security so that young people leaving education find it disproportionately difficult to find jobs; at the end of 1978 persons under 25 years made up about 70 per cent of the total numbers on relief work. This might have been a factor contributing to high rates of recruitment to the gymnasium and higher education. The standard of living has, however, risen within a mixed economy which also demands a great deal from its citizens in taxation, both direct and indirect. Public consumption and investment as a percentage of the gross domestic product rose from 25 per cent in 1965 to over 35 per cent in 1977.(2)

Although there are indices of declining labour mobility, a standstill in growth of productivity in the last couple of years, and more absenteeism of young people in industry, stability prevailed through a period of considerable social and economic readjustment. There has been a rapid shift towards the service industries and large manufacturing plants, together with migration from the countryside and from other countries into Sweden. The policies for education

---

1) OECD Economic Surveys, Sweden, Paris, 1979.
2) This was the situation as we saw it early in 1979. We are aware that in the meantime significant changes have taken place. (See the OECD Economic Survey for 1980.)

reflect in part the likely development of the Swedish economy. Sweden has to live in a changed European and world economy and to maintain its competitiveness through high skills and sophisticated products.

The investment in education by the Swedish people has been and remains large. In 1979-80 government expenditure on education will have amounted to SK 10.8 billion or 8.3 per cent of its total budget. In 1978-79 government and local authority expenditures combined amounted to SK 25.3 billion or 6.5 per cent of the GNP. A study covering the year 1974-75 placed Sweden among the most generous providers of education in the world.(1)

In spite of the many difficulties to which we shall have to refer in this report, in the view of one leading observer (2) of the national scene, there is continuity of expectation: "The dominating characteristic of contemporary Swedish youth is one of inter-generational stability. The young generation, through all its normal turbulence of puberty and adolescence, accepts socialisation into attitudes and behaviour patterns very similar to that of its parents ...". The lines of cleavage are mainly between political parties and social strata rather than between generations. There are, in fact, signs of some alienation of the young from the Social Democratic Party which was in power between 1934 and 1976; they tend to identify it with big industry, with life in the city, with high taxes and bureaucracy. University and college students were, in the recent past, as with their contemporaries elsewhere, caught up by a wave of radicalism. They have now swung back to more traditional attitudes, though some of them are open to the viewpoints of a wider span of minority groups.

There are indeed curious ambivalences that can be observed. Alienation from the school and deviance are often spoken about and may be associated with the lengthening of school experience, the distance between the school and society and the counter-attractions of the youth culture, as much as with such criticised characteristics as the teacher domination documented in the Swedish Background Report. At the same time, the opinion polls reveal conservatism on such issues as the abolition of marks or grades in schooling which have been advanced so vigorously by the trade unions, the National Board of Education and other parts of the official system; for the most part, pupils have inherited the attitudes of their parents towards education and society. The trade unions are alarmed by the growing passivity to

---

1) F.G. Castle and R.D. McKinlay: "Public Welfare Provision: Scandinavia, and the Sheer Futility of the Sociological Approach to Politics", British Journal of Political Science, Vol. 9, Part 2, April 1979.

2) Gösta Rehn, Education and Youth Employment in Sweden (forthcoming), a study prepared for the Carnegie Council for Research in Higher Education, Berkeley, 1979.

them among working class youth. Yet voluntary adult education movements continue to grow, even at a time when access to the gymnasium and higher education is so much more open than only just a few years ago.

The achievements of Swedish civilisation are impressive. In 1974 Sweden had, with Iceland, the lowest rate of infant mortality and the second highest gross domestic product per capita in the world. At the same time, however, we must also record some serious signs of social deviance as revealed by official statistics. Between 1950 and 1975 arrests for drunkenness among young males went up from over 26 to over 40 per thousand. Between 1955 and 1976 suicides went up from 27.2 per 100,000 to a peak of 31.1; they then, however, returned to a low of 26.6 per 100,000 of the male population. The corresponding figures for women were 8.5 up to 13.2 and down again to 11.4. Here we do not identify social trends in Sweden as extraordinary. What must be noted, however, is that a country that has invested so much in its youth does not thereby escape secular trends in deviance and social misfortune.

Yet the record of systematic social achievement as represented by education is massively impressive. In 1950 the great majority of children remained at school until 14. Perhaps 10 per cent continued in the realskola (1) or other selective schools and a smaller proportion went from there to the gymnasium. Now all young people remain at school until 16; 87 per cent eventually go on to two-, three- or four-year courses in the gymnasium. Many students who cannot go directly to the gymnasium do so after spending two or three years in work and many of the much older generation can do the same. Twenty per cent go to post-gymnasium education in universities or colleges. This figure is expected to reach 30 per cent eventually. An organisationally integrated, comprehensive and well endowed education system is thus available for all children and young persons from the age of seven until the age of 18 or 19 and beyond. Simultaneously, the Swedish authorities have increased and systematised opportunities for adults, particularly those who could not get access to more than limited education in their formative years. Special dispensations for entry to higher education are provided for those who have completed at least four years of work beyond their initial schooling and those who have studied at folk high schools.

2. CONFORMITY AND CONSENSUS

Sweden has thus determinedly created an explicitly egalitarian and unified system over the last 20 years or so. The reforms have rested on the belief that policies should be carried through on behalf

---
1) Lower secondary school.

of the whole population and that conformity to a national policy is
desirable throughout. The system for making and carrying out national
decisions assumes that consensus can be reached on objectives through
the preliminary work undertaken by national commissions, and that once
decisions are taken by the Riksdag and promulgated through government
ordinances, the system will work in deference to the national decision.
And to a remarkable degree, the consensus holds. We could hardly find
a practitioner, administrator or politician of any party associated
with education who was now against the general intent and scope of the
recent reforms. Disagreements arise on substantive effects rather
than on principles, on such issues as the operation of the rules of
access to higher education or the grading systems in the grundskola (1)
and the gymnasium, how to balance activities between research and
teaching in higher education, and on the effectiveness of its new decentralised structures. None would go back to a selective school
structure. No one argues the case for publicly supported private
schools. All accept that the period of large-scale expansion is over,
but none argue that education is a poor social investment. There is
general parliamentary support for educational expenditure. Dissent is
intra-familial in style and content. Parental and employer discontent
with the results of the reformed system is certainly expressed in the
newspapers and, indeed, it was expressed to us in such private conversations as our timetable allowed us to enjoy. But there is little
coherent articulation of dissent, and none who feel that dissent needs
ways by which it can be differently articulated.

3. THE DILEMMAS OF SOCIAL REFORM

Sweden has gone through the same stages as many other societies
seeking to equalise their social delivery systems. Until the late
1950s, Sweden possessed an education system in which inequalities of
class and sex and between regions were serious. They thus adopted
policies leading to an equal and integrated education system. The
creation of the all-through grundskola brought with it a strong move
towards centralisation in the cause of reform. But, as many other
countries have found, no matter how serious and committed the intentions of government, planning and increased investment do not, of
themselves, bring about deep-seated social reform. The Background
Report records criticisms of the Swedish school made in the first
half of the 1970s as follows:

> "The new curricula for the compulsory and upper secondary
> schools had not had the desired effect. In the compulsory
> comprehensive school pupils showed various symptoms of
> weariness and lack of motivation. The percentage of dropouts

1) Compulsory school.

rose. Fewer pupils sought entry to the upper secondary schools than had been planned. The pupils showed the same ties to sex roles and social background as before in choosing courses and paths of study. Enquiries showed that many of the pupils not starting upper secondary studies had negative experiences of study in the compulsory school and, therefore, quite simply did not wish to continue. The growing unemployment among young people gave emphasis to the seriousness of the problems. It was pointed out that the extended and more theoretical schooling had meant that young persons were isolated from the community and working life ... It was held that the present school is marked by teaching situations built around words ... that school is governed to too great an extent by the demands of higher education and not by the demands of working life". (Section 4.3.2, pp. 69-70).

These judgements are significant because, in Sweden more than elsewhere, the drive towards equality has been determined and strongly sanctioned by public opinion through the electoral success of the party most committed to equality. In Sweden, even less than in other countries, social engineering has no alibi. The drive was not made within a hostile political or social environment.

The Swedish experience, in fact, points to the difficulty of achieving change at the individual pupil, parent and teacher level by changes in structure, no matter how resolutely attempted. The change in electoral allegiances has been attributed to a growth of feeling that government is too ambitious, that aspirations to collective omnipotence have led to a certain insensitivity to the impact of the best-laid plans, that too much attention has been paid to structure and too little to the quality of life. So consensus now moves towards insisting that equality of provision must be accompanied by concern for the individual and for the rights of all to participate in decision-making. The consensus created by the work of government-appointed commissions, by the Ministry and by the two national boards (1) might then, it is hoped, begin to work better because adopted as their own by those who receive the benefits. So anxieties about impact and recipience are beginning to be expressed. As yet, these anxieties are somewhat weakly formulated and, in our view, not completely met by proposals for decentralisation.

4. THE STAGES OF REFORM

We can thus identify three stages of Swedish reform. The first was that of large-scale social engineering in which consensually

1) The National Board of Education and the National Board of Universities and Colleges.

adopted objectives were promulgated and put into effect through changes in structure, through equalisation schemes, through centrally-devised changes in educational content.

In the second and present stage the strongly centralised system is giving way to different patterns of decentralisation, in the hope that the commitment to change will find stronger expression at the working levels. This is, we feel, a stage of what might be called formal decentralisation.

The third stage might be that of developing commitment to reform at the individual pupil, teacher and school level in which there is psychological release from both the crippling effects of a socially divided system and from the side effects of the somewhat paternalistic and nationally communal policy which attempted to heal social division. Central decision-making thus gives scope for local action. The main intention of the social engineering stage was to create equality of opportunity, access and treatment. The main effort in the decentralisation phase is to ensure that individuals and groups in Swedish society receive what they need from education according to individual potential and background. Yet the dangers of this phase are already obvious. Decentralisation may return authority to some of those who would make education unequal. It may import parochialism. It may induce more rather than less authoritarianism by locating power in the hands of small groups nearer the point of action. These problems may arise, in different forms, in the newly established systems in both schools and higher education.

In both schools and higher education we see, therefore, evidence of Sweden's ability to change decisively its political and planning structures. The objectives are both egalitarian and liberal. Far wider groups might participate in educational decision-making. But the balance of power between teachers, parents, students and pupils, between them and the politically sanctioned system, and between the schools and colleges, the trade unions and employers is not yet clear. Hard work and thought might be needed to make the new arrangements work so as to meet multiple and potentially conflicting objectives: national norms of equality; local and individual participation; and beneficial impact on individuals.

The critic might say that Swedish educational policy-making still relies heavily on the specification of objectives, on detailed prescriptions, although the power of the centre has been reduced. The objectives may all be desirable in themselves, but the Swedes are left with a certain bewilderment that good things do not necessarily emerge from good plans and good intentions alone. There might be still too much emphasis on the discernible products of education. The intimate relationship between good process and product, and an analysis of what makes for good educational process, are still lacking. Attempts greatly to improve in-service training of teachers, to increase local participation in decision-making and pupil participation in the educational processes, to increase the social sensitivity of education, are all on record. But how these good intentions and good programmes will lead to genuine change are still questions that elude answers.

The Swedes have, indeed, attempted difficult tasks. They have regarded education as a lever of social improvement for both the individual and for the whole society. They hoped it would be an integrative force, not only through its ability to socialise all of their people into generally accepted norms of behaviour and shared culture, but because they hoped, too, that it would be possible to affect all levels of society, whether public and collective, or private and individual, or central or local. The public effort has been to define goals and to make large investments to be shared between central and local levels. The private effort has been through the contribution of taxes, but also through supporting consensually created goals by the active individual use of educational institutions. But the system has constantly to redress the balance between these different zones of activity and express an overall concern that activity and impact will be secured throughout all groups. Such complex efforts are bound to encounter uncertainty. It takes time for investment in the young to manifest itself in the level of adult society. And there are many other factors affecting individual behaviour that may have a stronger impact on social change, such as movements in the economy, or the activities of the media.

5. OUR MAIN THEMES

Before we embark on our critique of Sweden's reforms, we briefly summarise the arguments which we will deploy, and the way in which our report is consequently structured. The Background Report centres its analysis on three main objectives by which the reforms can be judged: equality; connection between education and working and social life; and decentralisation and democratisation. As the document itself remarks, each of these objectives is capable of being treated as an objective or as an input or as a means to reaching one or more of the other objectives.

The Swedish authorities' framework of argument does, indeed, enable us to treat matters thematically rather than by paying attention to substantive detail. We follow them in extending the analysis so as to raise questions about what might be done next. The best way that we can do this is to state each of the declared objectives alongside potentially conflicting objectives. So in Chapter III we examine how far equality has been achieved in both general and particular terms through, for example, the common school, higher education reform, adult and recurrent education and education for immigrants. We also juxtapose our evaluation of the large-scale measures to promote equality alongside their potential for individual satisfaction and other impacts that egalitarian measures might have on the individual. Similarly, in Chapter IV, we discuss how far democracy can be entailed in educational reform, and how far education relates to the world outside itself, while also raising the question as to how far education might legitimately sponsor individual rights that might not easily be accommodated with larger-scale change in society, an issue implied in the Swedish Background Report itself. And, again, we pursue these points of principle through commenting on the assumptions made in that Report and on the evidence and impressions derived from our visit. In Chapter V we take up similar potential antinomies for the content and internal organisation of the curriculum. In Chapter VI we discuss the centralised system, the moves towards decentralisation and the concomitant danger that authoritarianism may not be removed by changing the locus of authority. We also consider how far it is possible for a system itself to induce change that implies decreasing dependence on the total system. Here, of course, the examples of decentralisation are relevant. And throughout, we are concerned to take further the arguments about policies that affect social structure, public organisation and investment, but that now need study in terms of the less definable, but salient issues of impact.

III

THE DRIVE TOWARDS EQUALITY

1. INCREASING ACCESS

No country has invested so much in equalising education as Sweden. The structure of the whole period of compulsory schooling is now thoroughly comprehensive. The great majority of pupils stay on voluntarily for at least part of the gymnasium cycle. Twenty per cent of the age group enters higher education and this figure is expected to rise rapidly to 30 per cent. Serious attempts are being made to reduce obstinate sex differentiations of educational take-up and subsequent roles. The rules for access to higher education attempt to redress the balance towards those who left school early and wish to take up higher education after at least four years at work. Educational opportunity is not dependent on geographical location, in spite of the difficulties in creating national equality in a country characterised by a long and wide land mass. Although the compulsory age of entry is seven, most children receive some pre-school education from the age of six, demand below that age being largely unsatisfied. Provision for equalising the opportunities of ethnic minorities is also impressive.

We do not need to repeat the facts so well deployed in "Goals for Educational Policy in Sweden", and particularly the first sections of Chapter 4 which deal with equality through education. The point from which Swedish reform started has been described as follows:

> "... In the 1940s ... by European standards, Sweden had a weak and backward school system ... Compulsory schooling ... lasted only 6 or 7 years, and after that came a number of schools at the lower secondary level providing further education for less than a quarter of the pupils. Only 10 per cent passed through the whole secondary school. Technical and vocational schooling were limited to a corresponding degree." (4.1, page 47.)

The Swedish authorities were determined to raise the general educational level and to democratise it by improving the educational opportunities of previously neglected groups. This was achieved by the creation of, first, the compulsory comprehensive all-through school (the grundskola), then the comprehensive upper secondary school (the gymnasium) and, more recently, the unified higher education system. The system of parallel schools was replaced by comprehensive schools. By the end of 1971-72, the last of the schools had become all-through and comprehensive grundskolan. At the next level, after compulsory schooling, the courses of study in the gymnasium, the continuation schools and most of the vocational schools were co-ordinated into a new integrated system, comprising a total of 23 lines of study and a large number of special courses. At present it is possible for between 85 and 92 per cent of 16-year-olds to move into the integrated upper secondary school which is available to all compulsory school pupils up to the age of 19. And since 1977 there is a unified higher education system with rules of access distinctively directed towards removing inter-generational and other inequalities of access.

Within these new structures, change towards which began in the 1950s, attempts have been made to ensure that both inter- and intra-institutional inequalities are removed. Since 1962 schools must give pupils free choice in the educational path they follow. The concepts "pass" and "fail" were formally removed from the compulsory school (although indications of "failure" remain in fact in the first two of a five-point scale) and repetition of the same grade has almost completely disappeared. Differentiation of pupils by ability is delayed as long as possible. They can choose between harder and easier courses in foreign languages and mathematics and choose additional subjects from the age of 13. The experience of the first years of the transitional period towards this stage produced surprising results. Instead of a third of the pupils in the ninth grade choosing the theoretically biased lines, half of the pupils did so. By the end of the 1960s, two out of three were choosing them. They were, in fact, keeping all of their options open for subsequent study in the gymnasium, as well as noting the frequent reference to theoretically biased lines when jobs were advertised.

The next stage of the equality drive is to be individualisation. As the Background Report remarks, the expansion of compulsory schooling has often been bought at the price of uncertainty about how education should be organised for young persons. Attempts to allow differentiation through alternative courses in, for example, mathematics and foreign languages, enable differential teacher/pupil ratios to be provided where necessary. But the choice of alternative courses has proved to be socially conditioned. Among pupils of the same ability in mathematics and foreign languages, those from the so-called lower classes tend to choose the easier alternative while their socially more favoured classmates choose the more difficult one. Similarly, whenever students are able to choose, as in grades 7 to 9, boys and girls choose differently. The boys choose technology while the girls choose art and home economics. The same applies to choices made in the gymnasium after the age of 16. The Swedes have tried as hard as they can to change the pattern of choices as determined by sexes. For example, quota systems have been used on a trial basis in pre-school teacher training since the autumn of 1971. Extensive programmes for changing the traditional role of the sexes through education have been drawn up by the central authorities.

2. SOCIAL DIFFERENTIATIONS REMAIN

Perhaps the biggest disappointment is that differences between social groups and choice of upper secondary studies have not sufficiently disappeared. Theoretically biased courses in the compulsory school offer the best prospects for theoretically biased studies in the upper secondary school; while some 75 per cent of children of parents with an academic education opt for them, the corresponding figure for the children of unskilled workers is 25 per cent. Considerable differences between social groups in choice of upper secondary studies remain. The differences that used to appear mainly between the upper middle class and the rest have become differences between both the upper and the lower middle classes on the one hand and the working classes on the other. Differences have moved downwards on the scale of marks, so that social background now has greater significance around and just above the average level where the transfer rate was previously of very little importance. There has been much more success in removing social differences in recruitment to theoretically biased upper secondary studies among pupils with the highest marks. But there is greater social distinction among pupils at lower levels of performance.

Social background thus remains decisive for continued studies after the period of compulsory schooling, except among the ablest. As so often, egalitarian policies reinforce meritocracy, although a higher level of education is reached through comprehensive schools for pupils from all social classes, including those who lacked opportunities previously.

The pull of the outside community, and the norms set by it, cannot be reduced by education alone. Social differentiation is still noted between schools and between classes in the schools. Expectations are mediated through peer and neighbourhood patterns. It thus becomes the more important to find out how to help pupils who, try as the education system might to avoid it, will continue to be differentiated by their schools and social class.

Structural changes are not by themselves able to eliminate social difference, although they are a necessary prerequisite.

The differences can be perpetuated when content and methods are still largely traditional, teacher-dominated and with a low degree of individual treatment of pupils. There is also little attention paid to the use of special compensatory programmes directed to specific social and cultural circumstances of children from lower social classes. Whilst Swedish educational reform has given people access to the school system, the values mediated by the schools might not be adapted to the cultural differences of the children who come together in the same school and in the same class. Sweden has moved on from problems of access to problems of developing the talent that now finds its way into the system.

3. SEX DIFFERENTIATION

Equal opportunity is now offered to all pupils regardless of social background, economic circumstances and place of residence. Strenuous attempts have been made, too, to reduce inequality between the sexes. Extensive programmes for changing the traditional stereotyping of the sexes through education have been drawn up by the authorities. Separate girls' schools were abolished with the introduction of the grundskola and classes are co-educational throughout. Boys and girls are taught woodwork and metalwork as well as textile handicrafts. Boys take domestic science courses. But, again, individual choice defeats policy intentions. In grades 7 to 9 boys tend to choose technology whilst girls more often choose art and home economics. In the gymnasium, girls predominantly choose nursing and clothing lines of study whilst boys choose motor mechanics, electrical and telecommunications and technical engineering. If, however, the traditional ideas of masculine and feminine roles remain, girls reach a higher educational level than they did twenty years ago and, whether or not the education system has contributed to it, the proportion of women who work is higher.

4. REGIONAL DISPARITIES

Sweden has taken exceptional steps to ensure that children and young people all over the country have equivalent opportunities no matter whether they live in cities or the most sparsely populated areas. Free transport, assistance with board and lodging, special grants to pupils who have to travel or live away from home, aim at increasing accessibility of education at all levels. The largest population growth has been in the larger urban areas to which populations moving from the north and some parts of the west came. These were the result of structural changes in the economy during the 1950s and 1960s. The pattern was broken as recession set in in 1971, and many former migrants returned to their home region. Since then migration has more often been directed towards nearby industrial towns. This was, at least in part, the result of active regional policies which stimulated industry in the regions. But in 1977-78 the larger urban centres have again attracted people from regions with high unemployment.

The effects of reform on regional opportunities have been partly evaluated. The key areas are at the post-secondary level since all pupils between 6 and 16 have access to education in pre-school facilities and in the grundskola. In higher education, as a result of the diffusion of educational facilities and migration, the proportion of students living within 50 km of an institution has increased: 65 per cent of students in 1972-73 came from areas less than 50 km away from education centres. Pressure on the established universities has been reduced and they have not been so overwhelmed by mass demand as they might otherwise have been, because new universities or university outposts have opened. The impact of the new measures is shown in that the newer centres recruit substantially higher proportions of students from social class 3 and a lower proportion from social class 1.

5. THE EDUCATION OF IMMIGRANTS

In its treatment of immigrants within the education service, Sweden demonstrates its determination to secure equality for all of its citizens. Swedish population growth has been slow: about 1.7 million since 1945, 30 per cent of that additional figure being attributed to immigrants. At the beginning of 1978 there were 430,000 foreign nationals in Sweden and about 270,000 immigrants who had acquired Swedish citizenship; 60 per cent of the foreigners came from Nordic countries, whilst 20 per cent were from the Mediterranean region. There are citizens of more than 130 countries living in Sweden.

Many other countries have had to face the challenge of assimilating new immigrant groups into their societies, but the Swedes have been more determined than most in rising to it. The Swedes have accepted that there will be groups speaking languages other than Swedish and with a different cultural background which they may want to retain. Many immigrants will return home and must therefore be given the opportunity of keeping in touch with and developing their own language and culture. It is thought to be the duty of educational institutions to cater for immigrants' particular needs and at the same time to enable Swedes to become accustomed to living with other cultural groups.

As in other countries, there have been different stages of policy for immigrants. In its first stages of encounter with new groups within the community, a liberal society usually adopts what has been called a "colour blind" policy. It is assumed that newcomers should, and will want to be, assimilated to the dominant culture and that all immigrants should be, therefore, Swedes first of all. But as minority groups grow, the home culture is given, if not an equal place, then certainly enough place for its survival and development alongside that of the dominant culture. In this, Swedish policy has been exemplary. Whilst knowledge of Swedish has been the priority since 1968, Sweden has developed the principle of freedom of choice and of partnership with the main immigrant groups. So special instruction in both Swedish and the native language have become co-existing objectives. We may fairly ask what will be the third stage. Even within the second stage, difficulties arise as some traditional patterns - for example, those associated with the place of women in society - become revealed as antithetical to the dominant culture. Ultimately, it may be that the security induced by acceptance of the home culture by the wider society will enable more immigrants to come into the dominant culture on terms of equality and thus themselves adopt life styles leading to less differentiation. But, if so, that will be as a result of their own knowledge and choice and not through the insistence of those from the dominant culture.

The policies have been strongly implemented. Instruction is given in about 50 languages in the grundskola and over 60 languages are represented by those receiving labour market training. At the same time, all immigrants are entitled to free Swedish lessons under the aegis of adult education associations and to nine weeks of Swedish instruction as part of labour market training in addition to paid leave in order to take them. Basic vocational courses are given in the gymnasia to immigrants in Stockholm and in other main centres. Municipalities receive state grants towards instruction in the home language, and in 1977 were mandated to organise instruction in pre-school home language training. Special grants are paid to home language study circles and grants are available for liaison interpreters for the adult education associations. Close contacts are sought by the schools with parents of immigrant students. In-service training for all teachers concerned with immigrants and other minorities is in increasing demand. Immigrant education has been a priority for NBE research and development funds in recent years.

The results are already impressive: 85 per cent of the adults attending basic education courses and about 15 per cent of those studying general subjects in municipally-provided education are immigrants. And the school curriculum has been adjusted to enable both immigrants and native-born Swedes to appreciate the advantages and problems of a multi-ethnic society. Immigrants suffer the disadvantages to be found elsewhere. They have a higher unemployment rate than native Swedes and there is already some anxiety about the growth of prejudice which the schools seek to combat. Thus, the draft curriculum for the grundskola states that Swedish children should know about patterns of life and culture and traditions in other civilisations besides their own, understand why immigrants have left their home countries and learn about the background from which they come. In all, the Swedish effort is considerable and committed and is incorporated in a long-term programme for action.

6. ACCESS TO HIGHER EDUCATION

The latest major drive towards equality has been in higher education, where the reforms have been thorough, determined and radical. Although they have gathered momentum over a long time, the reforms finally implemented in 1977 were primarily the product of the Education Commission of 1968 (U-68). All post-secondary education now forms part of a unitary system (except for some functions residually remaining with the municipalities but likely to be fully incorporated soon) delegated through two main administrative channels and the regional boards (Chapter VI, Sections 6 and 7). Until comparatively recently there were only a few elite universities and other institutions catering for a small minority. Access grew until 1968-69, when it amounted to 25 per cent of 20-year-olds as compared with 12 per cent in 1960-61. It then declined for a few years but is now rising to its earlier peak. Age distribution has changed. In 1974-75, 39 per cent of those registering were above 25 compared with 10 per cent in 1964-65. Yet, although the proportion of working class entrants has increased, they number only 10 per cent (from nearly half the population) as against 80 per cent admissions from the most socially favoured twentieth of the population. The changes are thus already having an impact, although the latest ones have still to work their way through the system.

7. ADMISSION RULES

Swedish higher education admission policy has been drastically redirected to meet specific social objectives. Whilst it has certainly been concerned to meet labour market requirements (a motive explicit in the proposals of the U-68 Commission's Report) and to increase the number of entrants so as to compensate for reduced age groups and a slackening of the proportion seeking admission, the changes have become increasingly determined by egalitarian motives, and particularly by the desire to reduce inter-generational inequalities.(1) So after cautious starts in the late 1960s to widen the eligibility rules for adults, access has been increasingly widened until, in 1977, four categories of students became eligible: those who had completed the two-year or three-year gymnasium education, or who had a certificate from a folk high school, or who were 25 years of age and had at least four years (previously five) of work experience. The last provision is, of course, the most important from the point of view of egalitarian policies.

The four categories compete in separate groups for a number of places proportionate to the number in each group. Selection is based on average marks or the results of aptitude tests and on points for job experience of at least 15 months and at most five years. This is a deliberate attempt to serve those who did not continue through upper secondary education early in their career.

Higher education is organised in general study programmes, grouping five vocational sectors, and these are established by Parliament which itself took this power from the government offices. A general plan, which is the base for a full degree course of the traditional kind, is drawn up for each line of studies by the central authority for higher education (the National Board of Universities and Colleges, NBUC). There are also, however, local and individual study programmes and separate courses funded by six newly-created regional boards for higher education. These may constitute a separate source of influence on higher education activity. A further provision in favour of late arrivals is that a ceiling (numerus clausus) has been imposed throughout to ensure that resources are not completely taken up by general courses. The expansion of more traditional, elite full-time courses is thus restricted so that there will be resources for the more fragmented courses designed for those who come to higher education later.

Although the policies have been building up over some time, the extent of social equalisation has not reached expectations. Indeed, social selection has increased among young people going on to traditional university study. Also, the study aspirations of students have become more limited so that many more are studying less. The universities have increasingly entered the domain of free adult education. 'The view may be taken that ... new problems arising in consequence (of widening access to higher education) and the supplementary measures required have been underestimated in Swedish educational planning.' (L. Kim)

Some are opposed to the reforms. The National Union of Students dislikes the numerus clausus and, indeed, the selection and access rules in general. Criticism has been particularly directed against

---

1) Lillemor Kim. "Widened Admission to Higher Education in Sweden (The 25/5 Scheme)". To be published in European Journal of Education.

the degree to which work experience is used as a basis for entrance. The Stockholm Student Union has publicly complained that persons who may have received low grades in upper secondary schools six or seven years ago can supplement their points by work experience, and that they take too many places which otherwise could have been used by younger gymnasium graduates with higher grades. There are also objections to a system which works in part by lottery when the number of qualified applicants in any of the four groups exceeds the places available, even though there is a continuing Parliamentary majority in its favour. Younger students may get their choice to come back to a university education later, but many feel this to be an unacceptable break in educational continuity. Admission to many single-subject courses and to three of the full degree programmes was free until July 1969 for everyone having the necessary background qualifications: no distinction was made between adults and those coming directly from the upper secondary school.

Many applaud the general principles underlying the reforms, particularly when taken in conjunction with proposals to connect higher education to the needs of working life and with the principle of co-determination (see below page 34). But it is being argued that new injustices are being created. We have heard such phrases as "the rules favour the part-timers and the dropouts who come back for a little culture". It is even being said that some professors may be reducing the standards required of those entering university, it being essential to keep up student numbers so as not to lose resources. It is also said that there are too many single courses and that they are of low quality: "popular subjects lasting only five or ten weeks which could be provided by the voluntary organisations". These changing orientations, it is said, affect the general quality of scholarship. There is too much large group teaching and no real attempt to change teaching methods to cater for the more mature students. The student body is felt to split between the younger and more academically motivated and the older students.

Some of these opinions are being expressed not only by members of university staff but also by student representatives who express anxiety equally about the prospects for research in Swedish universities, a point which we shall refer to later. There is also the problem of the university teacher who is not allowed by contract, or is not given time, to do research although the traditional division between the lektor and the docent or researcher is about to be modified. It is said that the reforms all add up to a bits and pieces approach to scholarship and academic development. They are associated with an anti-intellectualism which partly derives from eco-movements, though they, particularly in Sweden, are also science-based, and explicitly demand that there shall be further research. A degree is no longer thought to be worth having in the way that it was, a point belied in part by the anxiety over admission to higher education by the parents of would-be applicants. Many people are admitted but then drop out after taking a minimal 20 points course. (A full degree course is 80 points.) The move towards equality has meant that many new institutions have been created which have little or no contact with research.

These criticisms come at a time when the new admission arrangements in their full form have operated for barely two years. The four categories of student for admission have applied for the same short period. The admission boards at the central and local level, which consist of representatives of "the public interest", the teachers and the students, have yet to be evaluated.

The main goal of the reform is "to create better conditions for a continuous self-renewal of Swedish education". The Swedish authorities state that the early stages will be characterised by unexpected and quite irregular patterns of behaviour by applicants, and warn against any kind of summary evaluation. They point out, rightly enough, that there will not be the desired return to study of adult students unless steps are taken to provide appropriate courses for them. Nor will the new forms of higher education come into being unless there is active participation by the new external representatives on the new planning boards. Thus, immediate effects are not good criteria against which to judge the reform. In particular, the new admission scheme will have cumulative effects so that the true outcome cannot be studied for some while.

It must be wise to delay evaluation of effects until the system has worked for some time. But it might be right to comment on the stated logic of the reform. Our apprehensions to some extent reflect more general concerns about the style of Swedish educational reforms. First, they are based upon a projection of desired social outcomes of equality and of renewal which derive from what is felt to be desired by the whole society. What is lacking is any associated analysis of the conditions which make for good teaching, learning, research and scholarship. Those conditions may impede the intended outcomes of the structural reform. If so, the authorities would have to face the fact that structure and academic conditions have to be changed through negotiation. Consensus cannot be assumed. Nor can the efficacy of management or legislative edict. Second, the principle of co-determination provides that those who generate the wealth upon which higher education must feed should also be represented in its control and management. But that principle, too, can be applied too mechanistically. The main actors in co-determination include those who work within whatever has to be co-determined. How, then, have the analysed needs of Swedish higher education teachers, researchers and students been brought into the formulation of these proposals? Has the consent of the trade union movement been thought more important than the consent of those whose own motivation is essential to the improvement, and self-renewal, of education? Third, the application of the numerus clausus will certainly help to ensure that the higher education system is capable of taking on the new challenges presented by the non-general courses. The forms open up access to many who would not otherwise have benefited from higher education. Yet the small numbers who are now excluded by the new admission policies, or whose entry is delayed, will feel aggrieved. Paradoxically enough, it feels more oppressive to exclude minorities than to exclude majorities. We hope that once the transitional period is over, it will be possible to reduce some of the pressure on quite able young people in the gymnasium who are finding it difficult to gain admission because of preferential treatment given to older candidates. Finally, we are led to ask whether some of the reforms are not examples of what has been called "the naming fallacy". Are all of the courses on offer really of university level? Differentiation of standards of what is provided in higher education is necessary and need not involve the creation of an artificially divided system. It is an excellent thing to offer less advanced and short courses, but scientific standards in teaching or research are not created simply by giving names to courses which mislead, through over-statement, both the providers and the recipients.

8. ADULT AND RECURRENT EDUCATION

About a third of Swedish adults are engaged in one form or another of education. Public support for adult education has been regarded as part of the process of social reform. The State has been concerned to eliminate obstacles in the way of underprivileged groups who wish to engage in studies. There is a wide variety of opportunities which have evolved over a long period. Nationally funded folk high schools, correspondence schools, radio courses, courses organised by employers and trade unions, labour market training (AMU), and a variety of education associations were joined in 1968 by municipally organised adult education. In all they provide adults with opportunities to study at levels corresponding to those of the compulsory comprehensive school and the gymnasium.

In 1975 legislation was passed entitling all employees to leave of absence for educational purposes. Assistance for adults undertaking long-term, short-term and part-time studies has been available since 1976. Trade unions receive state subsidies towards their educational and other activities at places of employment, and an experimental scheme of outreach activities at the work-place and in housing areas has been started. Sweden has thus fully embraced the principle of recurrent education. The aim is to enhance the ability of the individual to alternate between periods of education and other occupations for the whole of his life. This should remove the differences between generations as well as refresh the work force for changing techniques in their working life.

Some aspects of Swedish adult education deserve particular mention. In 1976-77, 289,000 study circles, sponsored by ten voluntary educational associations, attracted no fewer than 2.7 million participants of whom slightly over half were women. This was a remarkably high rate of participation; at the time the adult population between 20 and 67 years was about 5 million. Priority is given to study circles for trade unions and immigrant groups and to study circles for the handicapped. There are also study circles at university level, potentially leading to credit points, that account for about 1 per cent of the total of participants. The study circles, and the folk high schools which represent a tradition different from that of the mainline education system, endorse voluntaryism and variety. They allow personal and private effort to be subsidised by the State and the municipalities.

Since 1968 local authorities have operated municipal adult schools which offer instruction within the curriculum for grades 7 to 9 of the grundskola and for the various gymnasium study lines and courses. Eligibility for leave of absence, from 1975, and the special adult study allowance, from 1976, have increased the proportion of day-time students. The municipal adult schools now enrol over 200,000 students a year. Since 1977, municipal adult education has been charged with emphasising basic education so that all adults will have a minimum standard of knowledge and skills. Municipal adult education has succeeded in recruiting a strikingly large proportion of under-educated participants. Many of the courses relate strongly to the basic training requirements in the majority of occupations. There is also labour market training (AMU) which is a means of regulating the labour market and reducing unemployment. It is intended to provide vocational training for persons who are unemployed or in danger of unemployment. This special form of training is, however, also available to others, for example, housewives or handicapped persons who wish to obtain gainful employment. AMU is an important factor in regional policy. It includes continuation courses. Theoretical and practical training of this kind serves to improve the job opportunities of various groups with longer training behind them. The National Board of Education and the Labour Market Board are jointly responsible for the AMU.

Among the most important forms of adult education are the folk high schools. There are 110 of them and they enable local providers to offer more varied programmes than any other part of the system. They embody the nineteenth-century tradition of residential adult education colleges. They derive their traditions from political and agrarian sources and have made a major contribution to concepts of

Swedish democracy. Their historical importance is illustrated by the fact that in 1918 whilst there were only 3,000 people in gymnasia in Sweden there were 2,000 in folk high schools. There are now training courses for their teachers which have formed part of university provision since 1970.

Overall, Sweden has made serious and concerted efforts to reduce the gap between the generations as the younger people benefit increasingly from wholesale social reform. The problems that remain are those of content and method. The Background Report makes it clear that the problems identified in the earlier examination by OECD remain. It is still not possible, it seems, fully to use the experiences, knowledge and skills of adults in education. The National Board of Education has made strong efforts to improve in-service training and the initial training of teachers in this area.

9. PRE-SCHOOL EDUCATION

With entry to compulsory education at seven years, Sweden is behind some other European countries in the amount of education given to children during their earlier and formative years. Municipalities are required to offer pre-school education from the age of six. They also are required to offer it to all children under the age of six who have special need for support, including residents in sparsely populated areas. In addition, they are obliged to draw up five-year expansion plans. But there are serious unsatisfied demands for pre-school education, and admission before the age of six has to be made on a priority basis and for a small minority only. Thus compensatory education in the earliest years is inadequately endorsed by a system which has created such strongly egalitarian structures in the compulsory years of schooling. There are no designated geographical areas of special need and the system works, in effect, by identifying particular groups such as immigrants, or those who have left school early, for particular help within the general system. Pre-school education and infant care are often given on the same premises as the grundskola, so that close links between the two can be established. But the provision is the responsibility of the municipalities under their welfare, rather than their educational, duties. This is all the more surprising since the regulations specify that trained pre-school teachers will be responsible for the classes, together with other staff. On the other hand, this difference in organisations may provide the pre-school with some independence of the greater education system and thus increase its pluralism, creativity and flexibility.

10. THE HANDICAPPED

Sweden has shown itself extremely adept at providing for those with special needs and for all ages. As we have already indicated, the help given to immigrants, for example, is particularly impressive. In policies towards the education of the handicapped, Sweden has been very generous. These are not only educated alongside their contemporaries, but are allowed, or perhaps expected, to do much of what their contemporaries do. Equality can be administered mechanistically and social integration does not automatically follow. The attendance of the handicapped in the same schools as non-handicapped prevents their social isolation and gives both groups the opportunity to work together without excluding some of them as a separate category in society. Experience must tell if the social aim can be reconciled with meeting the specific functional needs of the education of the handicapped.

11. SOME GENERAL POINTS ABOUT THE DRIVE TOWARDS EQUALITY

Sweden's efforts to redress inequality have been remarkable. Nevertheless, the authorities are left with deeply perplexing problems which outside observers perceive. How is it possible to move forward from equality of access through equality of take-up towards equality in individual participation and development? The Swedish Background Report refers to this shift in the meaning of the concept of equality between the 1950s and now. It is no longer confined to equal opportunity to compete. Nor does it mean that everyone receives the same education, although all should acquire basic competences and skills so as to function as active and contributory members of society. "But how individuals develop beyond this, which is also a responsibility of society, is less concerned with equality ... Equality becomes synonymous with freedom from deficiencies, and (with) basic competence". In these statements, however, we identify an uncertainty in the Swedish approach to social justice. The Swedes are rightly anxious that individualisation and administrative decentralisation should not lead back to structural inequalities in the education system. At the same time, however, they are worried, as are all modern industrialised countries, by evidence of alienation from school life among those whom educational reform has been designed to benefit. It seems, then, that a civilised society which seeks to eliminate structural inequality may introduce new problems if the individual remains enclosed within a system which may be "equal" but which cannot take account of his particular needs.

In Swedish education there is a concern for justice and almost all of the documentation starts with social values, which, it is assumed are consensually endorsed. Not much is said about the ways in which individuals develop or the way in which the individual will see his place in an equal and human society. A rigidity is introduced when it is assumed that age and achievement can be closely matched and that curriculum and organisation can be homogeneous. Educational reform has been achieved by creating new organisational structures and then by adopting prescriptive statements about what should go into the curriculum. In the early 1960s it was to be English as a second language for everybody. Now at the later stages of the grundskola it is to be typewriting for everybody. There is, indeed, so strong a concern with global outcomes "for everybody" that the school's, the teacher's and the pupils' right to be treated differentially is resisted. The schools seem somewhat frightened of treating individual pupils differentially. At the same time, it is alleged that many of the more able students are being held back, although the International Association for the Evaluation of Educational Achievement (IEA) study refutes this. There is still concern to establish pedagogic certainty and uniformity in spite of many public policy attempts to the contrary. The classroom is said to be teacher-dominated so that individuals cannot move on by themselves. This was confirmed to us in discussions with gymnasium pupils, who maintained that there is too much teaching and not enough time for individual reading and work in the gymnasium. But if the teacher dominates the pupil, so too do the received curriculum and the national guidelines dominate teachers — although it is said, and we have no reason to disbelieve this, that there has been a great relaxation of control in the last few years. There is, nonetheless, a need to move more decisively towards reflexive rather than handed-on concepts of equality and, indeed, the conservatism of the classroom is a barrier to it.

Equality as a concept and as a practice goes through different stages. First, there is the removal of separate or parallel schools. Then within the schools the more latent examples of differentiation through systematic streaming are removed. Then, as in Sweden now, options and courses available to pupils need to be so arranged that inequality cannot be asserted through the exercise of choices that mark out pupils according to social origins and socially-endorsed predictions of futures. Finally, equality is truly reached when individuals are able to seek and work out their own destinies within a commonly provided framework. But within this succession there is a built-in paradox. Individualised equality ultimately leads to the maximum of individual choice which may then incur the risk of re-introducing inequality. Choices may coincide and will do so if the range of possible choices is not unlimited. The system by which choice is made possible can itself change, as teachers help pupils into a wider network of educational and other facilities. The challenge for the teacher lies in efforts to balance individual attention, at the level of teacher-pupil relations, with the formation of the collective group, at the level of the relationships both between teachers and pupils and among pupils. The collective groupings must then become productive and creative through getting on with tasks and not simply adhering together for "social" purposes.

In making these criticisms of the ways in which Sweden has approached equality, we are well aware that the Swedes, more than most, have pushed on from the mechanistic adoption of structures towards attempts to improve the work of the schools for all of their pupils. The first stages of equality abolished separate schools, streaming and differentiation. There are preconditions for the final stage of individualisation. Certainly, the financing of students for adult and recurrent education is extremely generous, so that rescue of those who missed earlier opportunities is more than a mere possibility. But concepts of social justice remain abstract and non-functional if they do not start from concepts of individual need and responses. Increasingly, the evaluation of social policies leads to an understanding of the difficulties of securing appropriate impact, no matter how well endowed and how well intentioned the schemes for change. Our doubts about Swedish reform do not derive from uncertainty about intention, or the sophistication and care of the planners, but about the sensitivity towards the impact on individuals that they reveal.(1)

---

1) In May 1979 Parliament passed a bill establishing a new curriculum for the comprehensive school to take effect from the academic year 1982-83. This curriculum goes far towards offering solutions to the problems and dilemmas raised in this chapter. In particular, it seeks to ensure that all pupils will acquire basic knowledge and skills, that one-third of the time at the senior level will be devoted to individually selected studies, that all pupils should have the same chance to proceed to the upper secondary level, that the traditional sex role pattern should be broken and that individual schools should have greater responsibility for the content of teaching.

IV

EDUCATION FOR DEMOCRACY AND WORKING LIFE

Education is a component of social policy in general for advancing equality and economic development. Yet educational institutions have a strong life of their own. In many societies, education and the professionals who run it seem able to create a self-contained province, a pedagogic vice-royalty. Education becomes an inner-motivated system which may abolish gross obstacles to access, which may change its own structures quite radically without necessarily bringing the content and style of schools and colleges in close touch either with general social norms or with the developing needs of groups and individuals in a changing society. At the same time, those who advocate educational reform have assumed, if they have not always openly stated, that there will be a spill-over from internal change in education to the external scene, or society in general.

The strength of much Swedish education policy is its recognition of the need to place education appropriately in its social context, to recognise that curriculum bears, or should bear, the impress of realities other than those perceived by the teaching profession. It recognises that the institutional structures themselves reflect and reinforce assumptions about education as a component of a society that must reflect democracy, the needs of the economy, and the need for social harmony. The Swedish Background Report is, in fact, quite critical of the outcome of efforts to remove some of the routine practices behind which education institutions shelter. We respect both the efforts made and the criticisms levelled.

Swedish education has attempted to make democracy a working concept in education, and education in its turn has contributed towards democracy through several ways. First, there have been attempts to change the content, style and ethos of the curriculum so as to make it compatible with stages of Swedish democracy. Second, there have been attempts to forge institutional links between education, at all levels, and the world of work and society in general. Third, the institutions and processes of educational government and administration have attempted to both import and influence democratic ways of working.

We shall be returning to questions of educational governance in Chapter V. Here we briefly evaluate what is being done in the first sets of policies.

1. DEMOCRATISATION OF EDUCATION

One of the most significant attempts to democratise education is contained in the 1976 Government Bill on working conditions in schools (SIA). It hoped to establish contacts between school and the community so that students should be able to grow into community life and school become "a living concern" to members of the community. Changes in school organisation were contemplated to produce an integrated school day in which traditional school work could alternate with other activities. Money could be provided to increase the number of teachers. Practical vocational orientation would be strengthened. And students would be able to choose alternative methods by which to receive compulsory education. The school would be democratised by the introduction of class committees in which all pupils would participate in the planning and implementation of teaching. A work unit conference would consist of all staff concerned with the work unit and an equal number of pupils. There would be a local management committee for every school (but this proposal has been postponed). The local school board would be able to influence the school activities in line with the decentralisation of authority from the centre.

Individual activity in the school would be strengthened and students would be encouraged to seek knowledge in society as a whole and not simply within the classroom. The curriculum would be revised for these purposes. There would be stronger vocational guidance. Co-operation between school, community and the labour market would be enhanced by the establishment of local councils for planning and co-ordination between schools and the labour market in every municipality. The planning councils would inform schools about the labour market and help them with vocational training. They would advise on questions concerning school work and on matters of working conditions and prospects. Schools are already being built so as to be used as community centres and this tendency would increase. Teacher training would include direct knowledge of working life. Provision has already been made to free teachers from school work for up to four weeks in industry.

The examining team feel that these are, again, strong efforts to change what has undoubtedly needed remedy. Traditional Swedish attitudes to education have been those of strong deference to the teaching profession, and have tended to sponsor the belief that knowledge is generated and transmitted by specialist educators. The SIA proposals, taken in conjunction with those for decentralisation, are certainly an attempt to move away from the notion of education as a product to be handed out by one generation to another. They assume education to be reflexive and interactive as a process.

We raise several questions about what is proposed.

First, we have received evidence from representatives of school students and of the Home and Schools Association that the spirit and intention of the SIA reforms are not being implemented because teacher attitudes, particularly as reflected through their trade unions, have not shifted (see Chapter VI). Certainly, all the arrangements for changing both the curriculum and the institutional arrangements will depend upon a decisive shift in the norms of individual teachers as well as on changes in planning for the whole system.

Second, we emphasise that education must meet several criteria at once. The practical aspects of education are not simply concerned with the acquisition of skill. They should require individual pupils to conceptualise and internalise their experiences. Intellectual and practical development is linked. Although there is nothing in Sweden's proposals for democratisation of education that is overtly anti-intellectual, the schools might reach a point where they so emphasise connections with work in society that they understate the importance of concept-forming and of cognitive development.

Third, the emphasis on the school's and the university's relationship with the world of work, of course, is important and healthy. But does the reform weaken the notion that to some extent education should build up viewpoints critical of the world of production and of that which is socially and consensually endorsed? Education must try to do both things simultaneously. It must encourage pupils to be productive members of society and to realise what the majority hold to be right. At the same time, it must enhance the individual's ability to be critical, to work so as to change or modify the consensus, to know that the full life is not only that which the economy and society at large endorse, but also that which the individual works out for himself. Some pupils whom we have met say "school is like prison", that traditional concepts of learning are too inert, and have almost a romantic view of work by comparison. The Swedish Background Report tells us that "Sweden has failed in one important thing in keeping up and developing child interest in learning". But demands for change must be sensitive in such a way as to present the student with life in all of its variety, including conflicting elements of that variety. So if skill training seems to conflict with other social functions of the school, the school must try to meet both and not emphasise one as against another. It needs not only to enhance the role of the labour market within education but also the role of the family and, indeed, of the peer group. In other words, we would be sorry to see the orthodoxy of traditional teaching replaced by orthodoxies derived from the obvious attraction of the labour market to youngsters who are apprehensive of unemployment. Nor would we like to see a perfectly appropriate insistence on the inculcation of basic skills, and of ways of applying knowledge and skills, reduce the belief in the value of aesthetics, literature, history and the development of concepts. These dangers are not explicit in what we have seen. It is really by strong emphasis on one side, rather than by attack on what we think to be equally important, that the Swedish documents give us cause for apprehension.

In raising these questions we greatly respect the intentions underlying the Swedish reforms. The school must certainly endorse learning by doing, through the emulation of realistic examples from the world of work and by reference to adult roles in the world of production and consumption beyond those of their own parents and teachers. The relationship between schools and working life is certainly not intended to be merely that of vocational choice and training. It is hoped, perhaps too optimistically, that work should be a place of learning. It can give concrete lessons, whereas schools can only be abstract. It can give glimpses of the adult roles to which all youngsters aspire, beyond the range offered by parents and teachers. It exemplifies organisational structures different from those of the schools and the families. Working life can reveal some of the mysteries of production and of the economy. And there ought to be some spill-over from what should be the civilised world of educational institutions into the working place. Criticism of society in both cases can be formulated on the basis of stronger facts and can flow both ways. It may well be that schools are overloaded with tasks which properly belong elsewhere. Young members of society learn not only from the schools but also on the job, or through the teaching given them by their colleagues in a work place. So when we allude to the dangers of anti-intellectualism, which can of course have its complement in academic arrogance, we are yet strongly sympathetic to the need - and the enormous potential - to make different groups more aware of what education is all about. These efforts require time to prove themselves. They need alliances within the school and alliances between the schools and the home and the places of work. School does and should loom large in the lives of young people as they grow up. We fully understand, however, the motives of the Swedish reformers as they bring the strength of the school into balance with the potential of the world of work.

2. THE VOCATIONAL CONTENT OF THE CURRICULUM AS PRESCRIBED

These intentions are important but their administration has to be sensitive. The integrated school day will involve the participation of people from outside the school so that a 60-minute lesson should not be taken as standard. But we note, nonetheless, the prescriptive nature of the compulsory school curriculum as drafted by the Swedish National Board of Education in the Information Document dated 14th April 1978.(1) This proposed: reductions in a subject to be renamed "pictorial studies"; reduction of the time allocated to music and Swedish; less time allotted at the senior level for optional subjects; practical education to be given an extra hour a week at the junior level; incorporation of economics and child-care in domestic science; typing, as we have noticed, to be compulsory for one hour a week at senior level; introduction of technology studies. Relationships with the outside world are provided for in draft syllabuses which will bring in the major problems of the society. There is at present a further proposal that the two weeks of compulsory work outside the school should be increased to six weeks, as well as a belief that all teachers should have spent at least 15 months in the world of work before they can qualify.

3. EDUCATION FOR THE LABOUR MARKET

The phrase "the needs of the labour market" appeared in many of our conversations in schools and elsewhere, and preparation for working life is stated as one of the goals of educational policy in documentation submitted to the OECD. The Swedish Background Report is, indeed, sensitive to the need not to attempt to mould education directly to a manpower planning function. Pupils themselves, as we have said, have caught the same mood when assuming that if the school is remote from the realities of working life, the world of work will remove all of their causes of discontent. Unusually, therefore, in a world where some trade union leaders at least have attacked the work ethic, Swedish education endorses work as a value in itself. This is, perhaps, the product of an economy which, in spite of some recent difficulties, has generally been successful in keeping its rate of inflation down and its rate of unemployment relatively low - even though it has affected the younger school leaver most. The more recent legislation, like the draft compulsory school curriculum, emphasises social and work aspects. It is said that efforts of education and training should be directed towards the major problem of youth unemployment. Relative unemployment is the highest among 16-19-year-olds, particularly among girls in this age group. Policies of connection between education and employment require mutual adaptation between education and working life. Every student who has completed upper secondary school should be prepared both for working life and further education.

---
1) Subsequently greatly modified by Parliament with a view to widening options and increasing local and school autonomy (see above, footnote, page 40).

These emphases on work and the labour market connection are to be found in both the grundskola and the gymnasium. Within the grundskola, vocational education is still trying to find its way. The education system used to provide separate schools leading to different vocational lines of employment. For good educational and social reasons the vocational element is now reasserting itself. There are systems for the counselling of pupils within the schools, as well as the connections with experience of employment and society outside the school already discussed. The Study and Vocational Guidance Schemes (SYO) in schools are not thought to have been as successful as was hoped, even though there is careful structuring of them with help from the Labour Market Board. Councils have been created for co-operation between schools and representatives of working life. And the municipalities follow up all school leavers for at least a two-year period. In the gymnasium many courses lead directly to work and some of them, including the unique four-year course for engineers, provide education and training leading directly to employment at quite high levels of technicians and craftsmen. Within the gymnasium we saw courses as varied as hairdressing, catering, work in retail shops, alongside courses preparing students for specialist undergraduate courses in physics or modern languages. Yet there is still anxiety that, as the comprehensive school system emphasises some of the other equalising and socialising functions of education, it too can easily become so theoretical that vocational education might be reduced in status. This problem demands imaginative attention.

Once young people enter the employment market, and much later in life as well, the education and labour market training systems provide several opportunities for both vertical mobility - promotion on the job - and horizontal mobility - facilities for training with a view to changing jobs.

The labour market itself is active in training. We saw one excellent example of a centre closely associated with a major Swedish industry in which, so it seemed to us, excellent help from a distinguished university was combined with enthusiastic sponsorship by employers, and active participation by leaders of local industry in the governing of a training centre. Whether or not these systems should be replaced by a synthesis of vocational education in school and in industry, as some maintain, is perhaps a matter for argument and further study. We have found hints that youth unemployment is lower in countries where vocational preparation is in more direct contact with working life and where the curriculum may be more flexible. In any event, one of the strengths of the system is the way in which those whose education has been primarily vocational have access to a wide range of higher education institutions. It is the intention to reduce the differences between general and vocational forms of education, making them more equal in status.

The relationship between the labour market and the education system is not confined to curriculum and ethos. They are reciprocal entities as recruiters of young people. It is thought that the high rate of recruitment to the gymnasium is in part a result of the difficulty experienced in finding jobs by those who leave school at 16. But this means that the gymnasium contains at least some unwilling clients likely to drop out at an early stage, or to cause bad disciplinary behaviour in classes. The attempts to provide counselling within the schools and the gymnasium, and to open up so many routes either through higher education provided by the universities and colleges or by the municipalities and the labour market itself are excellent. The adoption of such devices as programme committees for work training schemes which foster connections with the schools, universities and industry is also admirable in itself. The fact that such committees employ as consultants teachers who are actively in touch with industry is also important. Although, today, the main bulk of vocational education and training takes place in public institutions, enterprises are to some extent still engaged in basic vocational education and training. A Commission on Training (1975) found that the interest in company training had recently grown considerably.

V

STRUCTURE, CONTENT AND METHODS

1. CHALLENGE TO TRADITIONAL CURRICULA

At the same time as Swedish policy has radically restructured the system, there have been strenuous efforts to improve and change curriculum. The prolongation of the compulsory period and the creation of the comprehensive nine-year school have been accompanied by the abolition of streaming, the reduction of assessments and evaluations, a rejection of the notion of failure, and attempts to connect education with working life. Yet the information in the Background Report points a contrast between the progressiveness of educational aspirations and the rigidity of school and classroom practice.

Traditional concepts of knowledge have been called into question and statements of objectives, as in the Background Report published in 1967, have emphasised the importance of the all-round social development of the individual. At the same time, the growth of knowledge has been important. But a study of work in grade 6 (Bidänge 1971-72) continues: "It is thus a rather traditional picture we find of the teacher training from his desk and pupils receiving instruction... The dominant activity is to pass on factual information, to provide reports and description requiring registration by the recipient." The International Association for the Evaluation of Educational Achievement (IEA) studies made in 1971 also speak of instruction from the teacher's desk as clearly the predominant method of working. A study made at Umeå on natural science teaching among 343 pupils at senior level of compulsory school showed that pupils have little influence over the choice of the subject matter but that teaching aids play a large part. Laboratory work is used as illustrative material, not as an investigative method of work. Other reports refer to the dominance of subject-based teaching. There is little attempt to integrate studies as between social and natural science. In science subjects, teaching is verbal and abstract rather than practical and concrete. Instruction in the Swedish language consists of isolated skill training having little connection with the live use of the language. Language skills are not developed through encouragement to use them in any meaningful way. Pressure for training in basic skills has led to a reinforcement

of mechanistic teaching. Insufficient consideration has been paid to
the connections between the ability to communicate, to work with others
and to understand the meaning of the subject matter.

There are gaps between the cultural habits of the home - and the
informal learning which it entails - and the formal learning of the
school. The school embodies predominantly middle-class modes of
speech (1) and behaviour and thus, it is thought, alienates working-
class pupils from it. (Note here the assumption that the school should
supplement the environment and not only serve as an antidote to it.)
Pupil-influence on the work of the school has increased during the
1970s through, for example, the creation of student councils, but
influence of these is mainly on recreational rather than educational
matters.

Attempts to reform through the adoption of educational technology,
based mainly on Skinner's theories, have produced the "tysta skolan"
(the silent school), in which the individual teacher's part is reduced
and teaching aids increase their control. Knowledge goals in specific
subjects have governed the work throughout, with the result that the
overall goals for compulsory education have failed. These statements,
incorporated in the Swedish Background Report, indicate the serious
nature of the self-critique that has been made.

2. ... AND TO WAYS OF WORKING

One study made in 1976 showed that disciplinary measures occupied
nearly 23 per cent of teachers' working time. Discipline problems are
reckoned to be great. Many with whom we have spoken, as well as the
Background Report, speak of pupils' "school weariness". Motivation
has fallen when compared with levels noted in the 1960s. About a
quarter of pupils in a group studied in 1972 expressed negative views
with regard to contentment in school and about a quarter of pupils in
grades 8 and 9 wished to leave. The IEA study showed that Swedish
pupils were generally more critical of study and working conditions
than pupils in other countries. Interest in the content of the curriculum was low. As the Swedish Background Report states, however, the
reasons might not simply be the abstract presentation of knowledge or
lack of association with social needs, but problems in society at
large. Moreover, we note that Swedish schools allow - even encourage -
pupils to voice their criticisms and opinions to a degree unusual
elsewhere.

The school system has attempted to make work in school meaningful to all pupils. The curriculum for the compulsory school is

---

1) A contrary view now expressed is that teachers themselves lack
mastery of basic skills.

intended to provide all pupils with a basic education providing such skills and knowledge, habits, attitudes and values as are needed for their personal development and for their ability to function in contemporary and future society as gainfully employed persons and citizens. So there are attempts to create a curriculum "closely connected with reality" and to proceed from the pupils' perceived needs and problems and their relevant experiences. There will be greater demands for knowledge and also a reappraisal of the meaning of knowledge. There will be more individualisation and co-operation, and influence and responsibility will be shared jointly with pupils. There will be investigatory and experimental work, and a problem-centred approach.

These analyses of problems and of their solution have important comparative bearings. In Britain and Australia, for example, there are some demands for movement in the opposite direction, a move away from investigatory and experimental work and from problem-based education and a return to the basic skills. The Swedish position is that work should be both co-operative, in that the knowledge of heterogenous groups in class is exploited, and yet that individualisation must be reinterpreted. Communication skills through different media are to be expanded. Work should be based on concrete observations and practical investigations of conditions in real life. The amount of manual work should be greater. At the same time, all pupils should learn to deal with theoretical concepts and theories explaining conditions and phenomena.

3. LEVELS OF ACHIEVEMENT

These statements of intent must be placed against the levels of achievement thought to be reached by the Swedish grundskola. The main sources are the extensive studies on the standards in schools in different countries carried out in the 1960s and 1970s in the International Association for the Evaluation of Educational Achievement Project. "In all essentials, they could disprove the opinion often put forward in the early 1970s that the standard of knowledge of pupils in the Swedish compulsory comprehensive and upper secondary schools was lower than among corresponding groups of pupils in comparable countries." Swedish pupils more than held their own. But they also showed that educational achievements were not yet good enough. Studies also showed, and this is highly significant, that the schools are more equal in Sweden than in other countries. Interschool variation is 15 per cent of the total variation in Sweden while in other countries it ranged from 25 per cent to 31 per cent. Thus the principle of equal provision has been successfully administered.

Other criteria are important. Swedish pupils have anti-authoritarian attitudes, good attitudes towards civil rights and liberties, are "just under the international average in their confidence in the interplay between politicians and public opinion", have the most positive attitude of all towards equal rights for women, and together with New Zealand, have the most positive attitude towards equal rights for different groups in society but are pessimistic about the possibility of natural science improving the human condition.

The Swedes put much into education and have been among the most optimistic about what education could do for individuals and for society. They are the prime case study of the strengths and limitations of social engineering. They now recognise that the manipulation of structure is not enough. Yet the outsider remains uncertain whether changes now being proposed are much more than a change in the level and units that are to be manipulated.

4. MODES OF CHANGE

Pupils themselves talk about education being dissociated from "real life". They are anxious to improve connections between life and society. They wish to make sure that good theoretical development in education is associated with relevance and has a practical base. They themselves point to the problems of teacher-dominated and over-centralised education. At the same time, however, we are not sure that the reform of these problems is starting at the right point. Increasingly, in social policy studies throughout the world, the limits of social engineering have become clear. That which is provided by a beneficent state may produce not only results that fall below expectations, but also a new set of disfunctions. It is more difficult to receive than to give. That benefit which results from a preconstruction of what is needed by others, rather than from a perception of need, benefit and development emanating from the individual himself, does not overcome the now well-documented phenomena of stigma, labelling, demotivation, lack of interest and alienation. In education there are so many active agents. Not only has the pupil to learn to be an agent of his own learning but so, too, must the teacher absorb the world of knowledge and skills, internalise them, and then be able to develop them as a process of interaction with the society in which he lives, the demands that that society sets him, the needs and demands of the pupils with whom he works, and his own internal needs for professional self-satisfaction and creativity. But that is a different model from the one traditionally emphasised in Swedish education. There, instead, it is not the reflective individual so much as the caring, compassionate and reflective society that has been the leading partner. Social objectives are promulgated nationally. From them are deduced a national

51

system of education. That system translates generalised values and objectives into more specific goals and educational procedures, including the role and behaviour of teachers. The process of decentralisation itself may simply produce the same model of collective action collectively administered and prescribed, but at a different level in the structure. So we have to ask whether freedom for the pupil to develop in relationship to both his own and his social needs will be achieved if corresponding degrees of teacher freedom and self-motivated responsibility are not induced. It is possible, of course, that pupil and teacher freedom are not mutually reinforcing. The problem is that so many benefits must be sought simultaneously.

5. THE ROLE OF TEACHERS, EDUCATION AND IN-SERVICE TRAINING

Some evidence of potential for change came to our attention during our visits. Thus, a strong national effort is being made to enhance in-service training. One person with whom we spoke, however, observed that much of the money will go into changes in institutions rather than into education itself. It is certainly important to teach heads how to exercise new and more participative roles as needed within the schools and the expanded centres in which they will operate. But relatively small amounts of money are going into ways of revivifying the curriculum in terms of the new and more participatory modes. For example, there is no evidence of concern for the ways in which the power of the mass media, notably television, affects the teacher.

The role of the teacher has been under-examined. Co-determination and decentralisation generally, the new role of the centre, all affect the teacher's status, functioning and power. Analysis of change at the micro level, and its effect on the creation and administration of the curriculum, would be an important component for monitoring and inducing change. We know that teachers increasingly participate in the development of curriculum material and make their choices among a range of text-books. It is not clear, however, whether the principle of co-determination and of workers' rights have fully been applied to the teaching profession. Some models of industrial democracy would say that since authority for the curriculum must be located somewhere, it should be located with those who have to develop and administer what goes on in the schools, namely the teachers. They could be under the ultimate control of the municipality, and of school governing bodies, in which social values are expressed and, if necessary, authoritatively insisted upon. But the prime movers in this model will be the teachers rather than somebody external to the prime agents of education.

6. UNITS OF ACTION AND DEVELOPMENT

A further problem is that of the somewhat mechanistic application of egalitarian principles. We have already referred to the sameness of teaching irrespective of pupils' ability and needs simply so that all may be treated alike. Prescription to the individual or to a minority, paradoxically, is more oppressive than prescription to a majority. In other words, we feel that the perception of the units of analysis and of action resulting from the analysis is incomplete. The basic unit of action in education is the relationship between the teacher and the pupil. From that basic point, the relationship of the teacher to the pupils as a collectivity, and the inter-pupil relations as well, can be taken into account and the superstructure of public accountability and responsiveness can be built. That so many teachers, we have been told, wish they were in some other form of employment is an index of the need for more teacher freedom and involvement. The schools have been subjected to enormous changes. There are few who resist the general purport of the reforms. The mechanisms of change, however, at both the school and the higher education levels, have not been thought through in enough detail in terms of the psychology of good education, of actual social change and of the capacity of teachers to endure rolling reform.

In making this criticism we emphasise that no country has tried harder both to get structure right and to achieve genuine change. The attempts to release control from the centre have been enormous. And the dangers entailed in it have to be faced. It is hoped that hitherto uniform systems will now begin to produce examples of creative excellence that will be disseminated through a system of informative research, of analysed description, of exemplary excellence that will show the way to change elsewhere. And it might be change that sticks because it has been hard won by individuals in the schools rather than produced through the cerebration of those responsible for the national consensus. As it is, Swedish education has been criticised for emphasising structure and global results. There has been a concern with discernible and measurable products rather than with enlivening and interactive process. There has been a concern with efficient and socially-just structures rather than with style and the psychic elements of change. There has been an emphasis on the strong power of a national education system to produce a just society rather than with the growth of consciousness associated with the community. There has been, in the past, a monopoly of education by the school system and those who run it, but there have been strong attempts recently to change this. There has been a concern with the excellence of public institutions, so well demonstrated by the beautiful design and quality of equipment in the schools rather than with a more spontaneous, interactive and personally involved quality of life. Now that this structure is so firmly laid, it needs to be opened up, in order to become more creative.

7. THE 1979 BILL

At this point we should briefly refer to some of the proposals for change contained in an Education Bill that was being presented to the Riksdag during the period when we were in Sweden. Pupils' choice generally will increase to about 30 per cent of their class time. And there will be attempts to change the ethos and working style of schools so as to enhance problem-solving and enquiry work, alongside the development of skills. Individuality and co-operation will go together. Work at the senior level of the grundskola is to be undertaken in undifferentiated groups. Individual pupils are thus to have more influence and more responsibility for their work at school. At the same time, the government recognises the need for changing teacher attitudes. There is to be an emphasis on the local development of working methods. The municipalities have had more power since 1971 but are believed to have made no radical use of their new possibilities. However, some opposition towards local development can be expected from teacher organisations and the trade unions generally who fear the diffusion of their power through decentralisation.

It is hoped that all of these reforms will remove some of the problems which we encountered, albeit briefly, as we visited the schools. There we found superb buildings and friendly relationships between teachers and pupils. But some of the pupils' statements of why they were "fed up" seemed to us to be almost conformist. So many said that they wanted school to be more related to work, a viewpoint which seems almost bizarre against the attempts of radicals in so many countries to disassociate education from skill training and work preparation. At the same time, however, the demonstration of the new freedoms seemed to us to be surprisingly weak. There seemed to be a great deal of concern about a modicum of progressivism such as using home base rooms for pupils in a grundskola or the emphasis on particular forms of practically related work (silöyd).

8. THE GRADING ISSUE

We were interested to see how the grading issue had become of such high political importance. Previously it has occurred in the 3rd, 6th, 7th and subsequent grades. The political parties were divided about changes to be made. Thus, Social Democrats were against grading in the grundskola but reluctantly accepted that it must occur in the 8th and 9th grades. The Communists were against it altogether. The Liberals believed it should be retained in the 8th and 9th grades until more work had been undertaken about the nature and possibilities of different forms of grading. There were attempts to move from the established five-point scale in the gymnasium towards more sensitive forms of grading. Generally, as elsewhere, the baleful effects of over-early and over-prescriptive forms of evaluation were being resisted and tested.

We can record, however, that all of those whom we encountered in the course of our visits seemed to believe that the creation of the grundskola and the methods of open access at other levels were necessary and right. But almost all spoke about the need to move forward from issues of structures towards improving the inner life of the school and the lot of the pupils within them. Basic uniformity over the whole country remained a basic objective. No danger was felt of "privatisation of education", which would not be acceptable socially.

9. THE GYMNASIUM

A commission is now considering the future of the gymnasium and we have been asked to concentrate primarily on the grundskola and higher education. It will be appropriate if we refer here to some of the principal issues at this level that now seem to be faced in Sweden. Although recruitment levels are reasonably high (about 80 per cent of the age group) so is the rate of drop-out. Since 1971 the gymnasium has been a comprehensive institution for pupils beyond the age of 16, with courses ranging from those who are going to enter the retail trade as shop assistants to those who will take a three-year course emphasising natural sciences and leading to medical school or one of the science faculties at the universities. The achievement, however, has been to bring within reach a vast range of opportunities for many students of all ages. No opportunity is lost forever because of the creation of the comprehensive gymnasium. Other countries that have found so much difficulty in cutting through the legal and institutional barriers between the upper forms of the secondary school and further education might look with envy at the integration of the upper secondary school in Sweden. The gymnasium provides 23 lines and about 450 specialised courses in all. They are grouped into arts and social subjects, economic subjects and technical and scientific subjects. Vocational lines take two years. But they receive a broader basic education than was provided in the former vocational schools.

All of the problems that used to affect lower secondary education are, however, to be found in the gymnasium. There is, first of all, the problem of drop-out and alienation to which we have already referred. As the grundskola becomes increasingly less differentiated, so options are removed until the last stages, so the gymnasium itself has to take on the questions of internal selection and differentiation. This becomes all the more important as the gymnasium obviously becomes a surrogate for an employment market that cannot accept all comers. "Flexibility and open access at one stage are always paid for at the next" we were told. The desire to combine general education with the essential prerequisites for higher studies is not easy to fulfil, and pedagogic and internal organisation problems arise. There are efforts to allow for more experimental work in natural sciences. The curriculum is to be varied according to the environments within which the different gymnasia find themselves. The number of free periods for pupils is to be increased. The proportion entering theoretical lines has gone down whilst the proportion entering social lines and special courses has gone up. Is this because the gymnasium is more comprehensive than its predecessors? Once again, however, the sex differentiation in take-up of subjects is correspondingly disproportionate.

Gymnasia must vary enormously throughout the country. We spoke to teachers and pupils in a few of them. Some of the problems referred to were the familiar complaints that work was sometimes too theoretical. To this, however, we can add a different complaint which might be in conflict with it. Some bright and ambitious students undoubtedly find that the work is not so much theoretical as stereotyped. Between the ages of 16 and 19 or 20 the abler pupils certainly need time in which to immerse themselves in their own reading, experimental work, writing and reflection. Yet pupils whom we met testified to the great difference in style from the grundskola. In one gymnasium plenty of individual and small group work was evident. At best, the comprehensive gymnasium is obviously a civilised and interesting society in its own right.

However, gymnasia, as with higher education institutions, may be comprehensive in constitution and structure but yet remain as multiple institutions in themselves. A gymnasium contains very many cultures. Pupils follow strongly different lines in spite of the elements of curriculum that might be in common. There is a wide range of teachers, which is reflected in the number of hours of pupil contact that different subjects impose, as well as the salary differentials. There is, inevitably, a wide range of qualifications from those who teach the "hard" academic subjects to those who are concerned with mainly reiterative skill training. We do not say that these inner differentiations are necessarily to be deplored. But there is, within the whole of the reformed Swedish education system, a general problem that has to be tackled. How much differentiation is tolerable? Should it not be recognised that education encompasses not only the meeting of individual pupil needs but also the practising of several different arts, several different disciplines and several different strengths? The art of the good reformer is not that of establishing uniformity but of creating general frameworks within which consistency to some leading principles can be endorsed whilst yet allowing diversity of style and excellence to develop within. It is perhaps this constructive use of ambiguity which Sweden, in its earnest intentions to do the best for everybody, at present lacks.

10. R & D AND IN-SERVICE TRAINING

Sweden has always depended on research and development as one of the known sources of its ideas and mechanisms of reform. The proposals for the grundskola were, after all, based on work by commissions which itself rested heavily upon research on the differential ability of school children and on controlled experiment undertaken first of all in Stockholm. The commissions and the Board of Education and the Board of Universities and Colleges have impressive R & D programmes evaluating different aspects of the ways in which the schools and higher education function, and the effects of different reform proposals.

We have, however, two questions to raise about R & D. First we wonder about the extent to which so strong a commissioned series of researches gives room for independent and critical enquiry into both the values underlying reforms and the effects of their introduction. Second, whilst we believe that much of the research is important and desirable, as, for example, on the creation of non-graded schools in remote areas (the PANG project at Uppsala),(1) or on the effect of different outreach activities in higher education or of the results of creating a new higher education complex at Orebro, or the ten interesting and well formulated evaluative projects on the new higher education structures, we feel that there are many other issues which could best be introduced by those who are not necessarily associated with the reform process. Thus, it would not be easy for the National Board of Universities and Colleges to undertake detailed and perhaps anthropological studies of the effect of introducing public interest members into so many levels of the governance of higher education. The impact on the professional norms of teachers as the municipalities rather than the National Board of Education become more dominant in establishing a pattern for the working life of the schools would be another example. The same criticism has been made, as we noted above, about the patterns of in-service training. A lot of money goes into evaluating changes in the overall system. How much of it will go into

---

1) PANG: Process Analysis of Non-Grading

the more detailed changes in the curriculum and in the way in which the teachers' role will change as the curriculum changes, we cannot discern.

The R & D efforts are formidable. Educational R & D is for the most part "decision oriented". More than three quarters of it is centrally administered by the two national educational boards. It began with research programmes initiated by the State commissions. The experiments conducted with the nine-year comprehensive school between 1950 and 1962 at the instance of the Board of Education were an important landmark. Between 1962 and 1978 the Board of Education increased its expenditure from SK 2 million to SK 36 million on R & D. The Board of Universities and Colleges has increased expenditure from SK 4 million to SK 20 million between 1969 and 1979. (This includes, however, staff development within the tertiary system.) In all of this, the fixed resources, researchers and research departments are limited and the variable resources are relatively large. Much of the investment is explicitly related to development work such as curriculum renewal or teaching aids or evaluative instruments. There is also an emphasis on the diffusion of results. The R & D programme is reiteratively examined and evaluated by external scientists, politicians and administrators. An educational committee attached to the Board of Education includes representatives of the political parties, the municipalities, educational research and teachers and students. And the Board of Universities and Colleges allots funds to pay for longer-ranging research on fundamental questions affecting the tertiary sector.

In view of these major investments, and the sensitivity of the administration to the need to bring in multiple viewpoints in planning research, it might seem overcritical to say that some important opportunities now need to be followed. The research system is based on the Swedish consensus model. R & D should improve systems. But research should also set up a critical stance, or one of counter-analysis. The Swedish authorities have said in several places, including in discussion with us, that the "linear" model of research (in which it is assumed that fundamental research can lead sequentially to applied research, development and dissemination), is seen not to work. They are anxious that research shall be part of a "network of learning". Yet since reforms are preceded by R & D efforts, and since those R & D efforts are themselves the outcome of consensually determined work on educational objectives in general, there is a particular role for independently financed research to provide the counter-analysis. The independent research institutes, the independent research councils and other private sources can support more research that is independent of public policy but yet relevant to the development of usefully critical approaches to it. The National Board of Education has financed 190 R & D projects. It is these which, in the main, have

formed the main flow of thought and intellectual constructs upon which
policy has moved. The claim is that these projects question existing
forms of education as well as help to specify goals. To their credit,
the Board of Education published in <u>Educational Research and Development at the National Board of Education</u>, 1976, an article by leading
researchers which raises questions about the ability of sponsored research to form a sufficiently critical approach to the policies and
practices of those who fund them. Consensus from the main social constituencies has been expressed through such deliberative measures as
the Swedish Commission, the intra-governmental committees upon which
representatives from the world outside are so carefully recruited.
But demands for change are primarily the result of disequilibrium
rather than of consensually created equilibrium.

11. HIGHER EDUCATION AND RESEARCH

We have been told that all teaching in higher education should be
backed by scientific research and the budget proposals for 1979-80
contain resources to reinforce research effort. We will come later
to the extent to which the reformed higher education system might be
capable of meeting that prescription. Certainly, the new organisation
for higher education attempts to implant research into all areas of
higher education. These attempts will extend to such subjects as
nursing and social work which have traditionally developed from practice rather than from science. The universities are increasingly expected to act as advisory resources to these new areas. Some leading
scientists and, indeed, student leaders, are uneasy about the current
uncertainties in research policy. Some students to whom we spoke feel
that Swedish research, which used to be first class, is now in danger
of deterioration. We certainly do not want to endorse that statement
but record it as an anxiety that needs to be noted. One major and
serious problem recognised by all is the failure of the research system to recruit able young people. Potential candidates see that it
is more profitable and challenging to find work outside the academic
institutions. Research apprenticeship is too long and the rewards
too uncertain at the end of the apprenticeship. Some leading scientists maintained that it is fundamental research, rather than that
which is produced ad hoc as a result of socially consensual processes,
which is more productive and in the end is socially useful. Research
allocations may be made by the faculties under the reformed system but
a great deal of work has to be done to end the serious division between
teaching and research. Lektors do not have time for research.
Professors are increasingly detached from undergraduate teaching.
The faculties themselves have not yet taken full grasp of their own

powers to advance research which is not dominated by central government funding and objectives. It is protested that the official reformers have disregarded the role that the universities play in the broadening and deepening of knowledge which is a necessary antecedent to the continued existence of further development of the humanistic and technological culture.(1) Yet another author (2) addresses himself to the question of how far research can be "steered". The issue raised here is how far research can free itself from managerial constraints exercised by those who fund it and at the same time be made more responsive to the main actors in the field where research operates.

We have great sympathy with the Swedish attempts to ensure that reform is based on scientific appraisal, even though the value judgements must always ultimately be political and social, that the research community should be thoroughly responsive to the needs of society in selection of problems, that fundamental research should remain with academics for decision but that it is for them to get their own decision-making systems into order so that good decisions can be made. But we feel that the structural causes of dissensus are under-estimated. It is well enough established in the literature on the relationship between science and government that public policy is a matter for collective interaction, conflict and resolution whereas scientific development is often individualistic in its working mode and tempo. The scientist is motivated by curiosity and the desire to create intellectual structure, whilst the social reformer is motivated by a determination to cause change at the global as well as the individual level. The norms need not be in conflict, but they might be different. That being so, the relationship has to be that of negotiation between parties whose norms are not identical. Quid pro quo's have to be offered. Scientists might well surrender time and effort devoted to their own cherished pursuits to help, at least in part, to deal with issues which society is confronting. But the return to the scientist might not only be the satisfaction of doing work which could be in itself interesting and rewarding to his curiosity, but also degrees of freedom for part of his time or of his career to pursue his own concerns. Such negotiation could happen, indeed, within a system of research commissioning. The building-up, however, of an independent system is essential to any society that wants its problems to be solved with the help of able, independently minded but socially committed individuals.

In this chapter, and in the previous one, we may seem to have carped at strong and serious attempts at reform. To every solution

---

1) T. Husén, "Swedish University Research at the Crossroads", <u>Minerva</u>, 14.4.

2) E. Dahlström, "Interaction between Practitioners and Social Scientists in Research and Development". Conference at Orebro, Sweden, 1978 (unpublished).

we seem to raise an objection. Perhaps we ought to try to clarify how we now see the Swedish position on curriculum and content and internal organisation. We acknowledge fully the traditional, elitist and over-academic nature of pre-reformed Swedish education. We recognise, as well, that aspects of that tradition were consonant with aspects of Swedish life that might be admired, such as a concern for due and rigorous process and for the traditional touchstones of the civilised life. Centralisation for purposes of equality could not, and did not, strongly attempt to loosen up the style and psychology of educational practice. There is now a serious realisation that in virtually every respect the school has to become reflective of the needs and feelings of the wider society, as well as of all its members.

This brings us, again, into a deep problem affecting all education systems that want to change. The dilemma is that if liberalisation and change are attempted resolutely by the central authority, the very effort might be negated by the fact that it is endorsed centrally. Statements of liberalism by government do not change teacher or student behaviour, despite the fact that teachers are supposed to be civil-servant-like in terms of loyalty - and students are supposed to be grateful. So the alternative process is to hope for change by pointing out how it might best be achieved by the main agents in the field, namely teachers and their pupils within the municipalities whilst changing the organisational and institutional structure so that the schools will be both freer from the abstractions of central control and yet more subject to the suggestions of local, parental, political and labour market opinion. As it is, we feel that the prescriptions for change from the centre have all been made and none of them can be faulted in the terms in which they are stated. It is much more the process of decentralisation and the detailed impact that it might have on teachers and pupils that yet needs to be worked through. Other societies have also had to face the problem of liberalising their education and it has, indeed, happened. When it does happen, however, there can then be the obverse problems of securing other desirable national objectives.

What we have to say applies, as well, to those other important elements of educational change, namely R & D for education and the creation of advisory services. National effectiveness must certainly be sought. The centre needs to encourage R & D and bring it to the attention of the system. The centre should also facilitate the communication of experiments and experience between schools that initiate changes on their own. The problem then is how to convert the system's messages into action by individuals in local schools.

VI

SOCIAL CHANGE AND POLICY-MAKING

1. RATIONALITY RATHER THAN AMBIGUITY

Swedish policy-making, in education as in other fields, is rationalistic, consensually based, and technocratic. Swedish administration has always been centralised, but the concern for equality reinforced the tendency towards uniformity. More than most, Swedish administration is based on the premise that public institutions can advance social good. The schools and the higher education establishments would be able to embody the best of moral, social and scientific truth and practice, and deliver them to the whole population through a publicly agreed, endorsed and legitimised system. Certainly, there has been little room for the ambiguity that other countries have entertained more willingly. That ambiguity rests on the fact that education is both a public and a private process. It is public both because finance comes from the public purse and because the schools have to reflect socially endorsed norms. Society at large, the economy, the political system, the training for life within society, are factors that form the social and collective functions of education. At the same time, however, education is for individuals and should enhance individual development. The individual works and lives more comfortably within the smaller and local groups and there are thus private and local values and practices which also have a legitimate place within education. It is not unfair to say that whilst Swedes have been sensitive to the need for both sets of values, the emphasis has been towards the communal, the collective and the social and away from the private, the individual and the idiosyncratic.

2. THE CENTRAL INSTITUTIONS

Institutional arrangements for the making of policy strongly reflect the ideological commitment to the larger society and the assumption that consensus can be, if not actually created, at least reinforced and expanded at the centre. In the past, Parliament itself has played a serious part in the vetting of educational policy to a degree unusual in most political systems. And with fragile minority governments, parliamentary intervention has been all the more decisive. Parliament formally determines the overall framework and indeed some of the content of education. Within the central government itself, the division of authority is quite complex. A very small Ministry of Education (with 175 employees) controls the mechanisms by which laws are proposed, budgets agreed, and major policies promulgated. The Ministry embodies the political element because it is led by the ministers who are accountable to government and to Parliament. But the Ministry has no direct control over the administrative and professionally-led infrastructures which, inevitably and rightly, are concerned with the continuing testing, development and carrying out of educational policies and practice. Indeed, a Minister who seeks to directly instruct a board is, technically, liable to impeachment.

If the Ministry introduces the political element into education so that allocations of values can be made by those who are politically empowered to do so, the relationship between democratically controlled politics and the professionals, the administrators and the technocrats is more complex. The National Board of Education (NBE) and the National Board of Universities and Colleges (NBUC) administer and develop, as well as propose policies for, the system as a whole. The National Board of Education compiles the curriculum and recommends working methods, reviews the curriculum, is responsible for R & D in schools, and retains responsibility for Schools of Education and other training units. It is the Board which works with the county councils, the municipalities, the schools, and administers what has hitherto been the strongly centralised curriculum. Equally, the NBUC, which is led by distinguished administrators rather than by the leading academics who used to occupy the role of Chancellor before 1968 has considerable influence on preparation of the proposals for allocations which are delivered to the Minister on September 1st each year for consideration in the following year's budget bill.

The origins of this diarchy are historical. It was thought necessary for education to be free from potential harassment by the monarchy. It was thought that the essentially professional tasks of thinking-through the curriculum and of making provision for its good administration should be in the hands of boards whose continuity would be guaranteed by lack of deference to a necessarily volatile political leadership. Yet, it could be asked whether it can be right that the leading value-setters in the Riksdag and the Ministry should be at one remove from the institutions where learning, teaching, research and other educational activities take place; those institutions might need a measure of protection from the vagaries of politics. The freedom enjoyed by the boards can mean that politics are indeed encountered by professionals within the boards working on their own terms. The system has worked well because education has been able to move forward consensually, particularly during a period of four decades of rule by one party. There is now, however, no explicit consensus and there is no guarantee that what the boards propose, ministers and the Riksdag will accept. Such issues as grading or the option schemes in schools are, surprisingly to some outsiders, matters of high controversy between the Board, the Ministry and the Riksdag even though we have been told that education policy now plays a greater role in public debate than it has done for a couple of decades.

Moreover, it might be noticed how the strength of the professional and technocrat has been weakened, paradoxically, by the very political consensus of which they form part. For once there was a change of political control the consensus between officials and ministers became less certain and the neutral status of the professionals might be impugned in the eyes of one political group by their very strength in a previous administration.

The points we make here do not seem to us to indicate an unhealthy fragmentation of authority. It is possible to put a positive construction on the system in terms of the development of open politics. It may well be that there should be continuing and fruitful tension between the political entity, elected through Parliament, and the professionals strongly established in highly efficient and centralised boards. That formula may work well as long as politics do become genuinely open throughout the whole system through decentralisation. Most, but not all, feel that the present structure, if strange to outsiders, works well.

3. ROLLING REFORM AND THE COMMISSIONS

The concept of rolling reform has become an internationally celebrated feature of the Swedish system. As the Background Report itself remarks, however, it has perhaps been overstated in importance. The intention was that powerful planning for education should be a self-changing system. The concept would not replace the traditional Swedish system of appointing commissions to evaluate and establish future policies, but should supplement it. The earlier OECD Report did, indeed, express the fear that a sophisticated system of rolling reform, incorporating the commissions, their reiterative study of objectives and the steering of changes in them, the supplementation of the system by powerful R & D investment, might enhance technocracy. It also asked whether reform activity might not be strongly internalised. The Swedish answer to this has been, characteristically, rational and drastic. If planning is strong, that is no bad thing, but it will now be accompanied by equally strong measures of decentralisation and democratisation, so that strong government is not centralised and oligarchical, but decentralised and polyarchic.

Government commissions have been powerful mechanisms through which government has elaborated and tested proposals for change. Hardly any major reform was not preceded by one. They will, it is certain, continue to be important, but may have to work in a different context as decentralisation and more open decision-making increase. Every democratic government uses a limited elite to advise it. There is value in having able and to some extent representative people from outside the government machine who can be used as sounding boards. But reliance on the commission system as a principal means of guaranteeing democratic airing of issues is insufficient. In earlier days, when the ballot box was seen to be sufficient guarantee of the democratic quality of a decision, they were certainly good enough. Now when dissensus rather than consensus must be assumed, when politics have to be open and analysis has to be followed by counter-analysis, the commission system might be seen as too elitist and also likely to preempt decisions before the politicians at the centre are able to make an impression on the proposals. The corporate system ensures that different groups are represented, but formal representation does not always convey the full range of practitioner and client opinion. They do not include the public at large and the non-teachers in the decisions that are being made. That may not be objectionable in itself so long as other forces are allowed to work on the decision-making process. It is also true, however, that new ministers do not hesitate to elaborate or change the terms of reference of commissions. Moreover, we certainly do not infer that there is any form of collusion between the committee system and the two powerful boards. Indeed, the Ministry has no funds with which to finance its own R & D. It cannot directly instruct the two boards. But it can set up commissions and can hope that research will be invoked by them.

4. DECENTRALISATION

If, then, centralisation and strong central consensus have been the dominating themes of the period of major reform, it is now accepted that the local and the individual, as well as the public and social world of education have to be reckoned with. Since 1976, there have been serious attempts to produce decentralisation. In common with most advanced welfare states, Sweden realises that there is a yawning gap between the statement of values and their implementation through action, that the principal change agents cannot always sustain that which they intend, that the impact of policies is uncertain until the clients and the recipients are educated to become active partners in, and agents of their own welfare. Thus the technical justification for decentralisation is to get closer to "where the action is" with increased probability of dialogue. And here, once again, the world has a great deal to learn from the problems which Swedish society now faces. For, in releasing control from the centre, other risks may come. Equality might come into hazard if education is strongly delegated to the 287 municipalities. Devolution to many decision-making centres can mean that atomism replaces centralism and the sense of national standards and quality is reduced. There is, too, the danger that professional leadership will be less competent in a decentralised system. These are risks well worth taking for the benefit that local initiative can bring. But the dangers need to be reckoned with as institutional structures are developed.

It is clear that much power has been devolved upon the communities, and this trend began some while ago. The administration of the schools belongs to the publicly-elected municipalities or communities. Decentralisation, however, raises sharp issues. Does decentralisation to the communities mean that there is devolution to the school? What, in fact, is the prime institution so far as educational decision-making is concerned? And if the school and its teachers have more power as compared with the central authorities, what are the resulting relationships between the professionals, their clients (the pupils) and the municipality? Is not yet a further act of decentralisation, towards a school governing body, now to be contemplated? If so, the costs will be great in time spent at meetings and the creation of another level of organisation. But benefits are likely to follow.

At the local level there can be conflicts of equally desirable positions. The State will continue to sustain reasonable uniformity of standards and public policies such as those of equality. The municipality can try to ensure that schools provide a good education for all citizens and are responsive to local needs and issues. The rectors of schools and their teachers can sustain high professional standards which enable the practitioner to be creative and to exercise a professional leadership role in developing curriculum. The parent, whose interest is so essential to the good functioning of a school, can become a partner in the school enterprise, as can, in a different way, the pupil. The difficulty is to create structures that take account of all of these functions and bring them together into a system that works. There is certainly a clear reluctance in Sweden to provide school governing bodies on the pattern of, say, Britain, where, increasingly, the parents of pupils at the school, and teachers, are all members of the governing body. That would not be accepted in Sweden, where the notion is much more that the head should be the chairman of a governing body which includes community representation. In addition, the idea is to increase the responsibility of pupils and students rather than to provide organisational structures that can be conceived as a kind of alliance (parent-teacher) against pupils.

5. TEACHER AND PARENT POWER

In Sweden, the teachers' unions have the right, according to the co-determination rules (MBL), to negotiate with the municipalities before any major changes affecting their work places may be introduced. They can also give views on the schedules of work, the use of resources, and working conditions at a particular school. They can make observations on promotions and other appointments and, as might be expected, often press the claims of seniority. They do not, however, have direct power to participate in decisions on appointments.

In this changing and complex situation it is interesting to note how other representative bodies are beginning to assert themselves. The National Federation of Parent-Teachers Associations now has some 1,900 local branches, representing the majority of households in which children are at school. They complain that since the publication of proposals based on a government report intended to reform the working life of the school, nothing has happened. The SIA reforms introduced in 1976 have been held up because of failure to reach agreements on the teacher's working day. Local authorities are said to be hesitant or negative for financial reasons. The Home and School Associations have pressed for many policies now formally adopted: that decision-making in the school must be decentralised and that staff and students and the parents of students must take a common responsibility for the development of their school. They say there needs to be better contact between individual homes and the school. There should be class meetings where pupils, parents and staff meet to discuss current issues and common work tasks. Schools should become closer to the community and accept that they are "the determining pedagogic environment". Parents are now brought into the school to talk about their work and, it is hoped, educated to help their children better. The decentralised local schools should function as a social system and not just as a pedagogical institution. The National Federation, it should be noted, undertakes projects of its own. For example, it has persuaded insurance companies to give quite a large sum for project work on the nature of and ways of coping with vandalism.

There are also two large associations of school students who have places on such bodies as the National Board of Education itself and on many of their working commissions. They take up many of the recreational functions of the school, but are also concerned that "teacher dominance" should be reduced and that pupils have a larger say in the running of the school. These activities are important in themselves no matter what one may think of particular attitudes on specific issues raised by them.

Teachers are often worried, everywhere, about the advancement of parental power. Swedish studies already show that if parents have influence on a school and on the code of its teachers, they are mainly upper and middle class parents and, indeed, mainly in areas dominated by upper and middle class families. They might form a "steering group" which creates a mutual understanding with teachers on norms to be adopted, even if teachers feel that pressure is being imposed upon them.

The Ministry of Education has drawn up proposals to increase the influence of pupils and parents in school. Local consultative and management committees might be set up at the level of a district or individual school and they should be composed of pupils, parents and staff. They will have the right to make decisions in some matters and be consulted on others. A decision on these proposals might be made during 1979. Perhaps we can emphasise, however, that the decisive change will come not by any "concessions" on the part of teachers, but by teachers appreciating that working with their clients, parents and pupils strengthens rather than weakens their role. For parents need to learn how to use their rights and how to become good clients. The head teacher of a school with a strong governing body has the task of interpreting and satisfying client wishes, of defending by social criteria the curricula that are worked out by the professionals, of exercising leadership with groups well beyond his own pupils so as to make the school more effective. Participation means an extension of the educator's role and not a restriction on it, unless a mechanistic interpretation of constitutional arrangements simply leads either to tokenism, in which only the powerless are sent as representatives, or to unnecessary confrontation.

6. HIGHER EDUCATION GOVERNANCE

Swedish higher education is important as an example of changing political control. In the past there was a control familiar to some other European countries, in which strong centralisation of both the curriculum and appointments was nonetheless operated through intensive consultation with, and dependence on, the judgement of the elite group of professors and other academics. Thus there was participation of some of the principal actors but not the students, the larger society, except inasmuch as they were represented by the central administrators, and the junior academic staff. On the basis of this limited and specialised participation, there was an astonishing degree of centralisation. The "general" courses, that is those leading to the award of a full degree, were subjected to centralised curriculum. If a university wished to deviate from the main lines of the national curriculum, agreement had to be secured among all of the universities working in that area. Sweden has not completely given up these mechanisms of control, but has seen, nonetheless, quite considerable decentralisation. New professorships, entailing new areas of study, have to be approved, even now, by Parliament and by admission boards consisting of a majority of representatives of "the public interest" and of teachers and of students. Parliament decides what general studies programmes are to be offered, their length and where they should be located. Once a year it votes a 30-item budget. The Ministry formulates the general proposals, but the National Board of Universities and Colleges is responsible in a more direct sense for allocation of resources and courses.

There is now delegation to two sets of institutions. First, each institution of higher education has a local board of higher education concerned with economic administration and planning, personnel matters and the like. Faculty boards and programme committees report to them. The local boards are not normally concerned with the details of course content. The programme committees are responsible for undergraduate degree programmes. The programme committees and the local boards of higher education are subject to the co-determination law. Programme committees include representatives of teachers, students and staff as well as the relevant professional areas. A university board has a chairman appointed by the government, six teachers, including the rector, three students, three other staff and six politicians. The faculty board has a chairman elected by the teachers. There are seven teachers, two students and two staff. A programme committee has four teachers, four students and one member of staff. In the department boards the chairman is appointed by the university board; there are five teachers, five students and one other member of staff. Thus professorial control has been dispersed not only among junior academics, students and other members of the universities and colleges, but among outside politically-nominated representatives.

7. THE REGIONAL BOARDS

The arrangements are complicated by the result of a political compromise, namely, the creation of six regional boards which match the areas covered by the six universities and 30 other educational units. Apart from general duties connected with the overall planning of higher education within each region, they have special responsibility for "single" course and for local and individual study lines for which they allocate money to different institutions out of a lump sum given each year. They thus have planning responsibilities which include some facilities under the authority of county councils and the municipalities. In these boards 14 members are appointed to represent various groups in society at large, whilst five members represent various academic interests.

There is, thus, a new system which is both decentralised and based on a corporate view of co-determination. Throughout, there is a determination that academic life will be affected by social considerations. So the regional boards, which have no direct influence on the traditional undergraduate teaching functions of the universities, nonetheless have an important impact on higher education institutions through their ability to give money for "single" line work (specialised courses not leading to a full degree). The regional boards are free to decide what to do with their money in this respect. And what they decide to allocate an institution is affected by the general lines which are determined centrally. The regions may certainly be active in ensuring that people from all communities get higher education, and that particular needs and problems of a region are reflected in the education offered and research initiated. It is they who promote distance courses.

Complaints about the regional boards are multiple and contradictory. Many think they simply impose a new level of bureaucracy. Others think there are too many members, some of whom perform a formal rather than a truly representative role. If there is conflict on a regional board, and many are still learning their way, it is likely to be over a question of geographic distribution of resources within a region rather than over a matter of academic balance, let alone ideology.

Some, although certainly not all, of the leading and most respected academics were in favour of a reorganisation which devolved control to the institutions themselves and made sure that curriculum development and resource allocation were responsive to student feeling and to the feelings of those outside the academic enterprise.

8. STUDENT CRITICISMS

On the overall scheme for decentralisation, some of the strongest opposition came from student leaders who felt that the reorganisation had led to serious damage to academic quality. Decentralisation had brought what they felt to be a false democratisation of higher education. Scientific standards were suffering as academic staff had to attend to the needs of new and less well qualified students entering higher education late in life. There was certainly a feeling, which we can record from sources other than those contacted during our visit as examiners, that academic authority to develop curriculum and research in a proper setting of academic freedom, albeit within centrally laid down guidelines, has now been weakened. The course boards might now represent anti-meritocratic sources, putting forward a particular view of a public interest, as against that of science, knowledge, research and learning. Equally, the dominance of trade union membership on the regional board was viewed by many, both within higher education and within the schools, with apprehension. It was felt that centralised trade unions who were inevitably concerned with sectional interests were there not to establish good working relationships in an area of human activity where individual creativity and initiative are important but, instead, to exert vetoing power for extrinsic reasons.

It would be presumptuous for outsiders to pass judgement on these matters. And co-operation with trade unions has proved productive in other spheres, such as where the law of co-determination has been an important line of agreement and compromise. Our anxiety can be narrowed down to two points, applying to both the schools and higher education decentralisation. First, there is insufficient attention being paid to the psychological conditions in which good educational work can take place. Education is labour intensive, and the quality of teaching and of research is directly related to job satisfaction and freedom to be creative and interactive. These qualities are not the product of legal prescription, but of inner motivation. Just as teacher dominance of the classroom echoes state dominance of the curriculum, so might defensive views result from systems intentionally democratic but operated without due deference to the need of the key worker in education - the teacher.

Swedish university teachers and researchers do not feel that their society cherishes them. If that is so, and we cannot judge, it would be a pity. Swedish science and organisational innovation have been among the leading world examples. So we press the need for research, analysis and public debate about the ways in which the self-confidence and willing self-motivated sense of responsibility and accountability can be restored to Swedish teachers of all levels. Second, however, we question whether the best way of making schools and higher education institutions responsive to society is to establish corporate mechanisms. The mechanisms have to be there. But does not the best way to partnership between the different groups lie in action to make all roles stronger rather than any of them weaker? In particular, we do not see that decentralisation will necessarily make the school into a viable working democracy in which teachers play a sufficiently responsible role. It is they who have to be firm enough to take the pressure, as they should, of client demand for a changing curriculum and for better standards. It is they who have to make generalised statements of objectives and turn them into working practices and curricula. Strong student, pupil and parent inputs have to be matched by strong professionalism. In this we feel that the resources being put into in-service training need to be increased. The teacher training system should increasingly become a strong consultant force which will make teachers more confident as professionals, through being responsive to pupil needs. In this way, too, the schools would be the starting point for educational research and development and not simply the recipients of its findings. In this model, local school boards, which we propose should be developed for each school, will have several functions. They will ensure participation of parents and pupils as well as of individual teachers in decision-making as a matter of democratic right. But they will also have a deep functional purpose of improving the education being provided. They will cause the teachers, through their sharing of decision-making with parents and pupils, to become the educators of parents and of their whole community. Teachers' tasks will become wider, and their role stronger rather than weaker. Within such a school framework the class, too, could become a stronger forum for democratic development. Such changes would mean moving away from a somewhat sterile concern with democratic institutions towards the type of ideal argued for Britain by John Stuart Mill in which he postulated the argument for democracy as an educative force.

This type of model would, we believe, help meet some of the anxieties expressed by the trade unions. They rightly argue the need for the schools and colleges to relate better to working life. We share their concern, but also share the concern of many of their ablest fellow citizens about the dangers of anti-intellectualism and of restricting the growth of teacher creativity. They speak about the danger that information might be dominated by employers. We agree, but also note the danger of education systems being dominated by many other particular groups. They are worried about the power of individual teachers to act discriminately against the less well endowed pupils. We agree, but say that society needs its teachers to use powers of discrimination based on confident interplay with the larger community.

9. CHANGING THE ROLE OF THE CENTRE

This brings us back to the power of the centre. It was central politicians and administrators who created a system which gave so many new opportunities to so many more Swedes. What should the centre do as decentralisation is built up? We feel that it has several important and new roles. Just as the senior academics and rectors of schools will need to take on an educative role with a far wider constituency because of decentralisation, so will the centre increasingly have to take on a role in which prescriptive authority becomes reduced while leadership power becomes enhanced. We believe that decentralisation could go even further in reducing the prescribing of curriculum from the centre, although common cores may be necessary because of pupil mobility. To be candid, some of the debates in the legislature seem to us to be simply not worthy of so detailed central decision-making. However, the monitoring and promulgation role needs to be enhanced. For example, we believe that different patterns of power relationship will develop from decentralisation. The centre should be actively studying them and informing the municipalities and higher education institutions about the alternative patterns, their merits and demerits. The R & D programmes already are major potential sources of information. Both boards have excellent dissemination procedures whereby publications of summaries of research are made freely available. They hold seminars where key people may discuss some of the major issues resulting from research and policy development. The centre could build up that system even more, with a view not only to disseminating R & D results but also so as to engage in discussion about the very many points of development, of curriculum design, of internal school organisation, of the developing governance and politics of education, as they arise from the experience of those in the schools and colleges themselves. In the past it has had to work by a process of disaggregation. That is to say, the generalised objectives and guidelines for practice have been deduced from social, educational and other objectives. It must now get into the business of collating the best practices and disseminating them so that they become the criteria by which others to whom power is now devolved may act. More specifically, the centre must give more attention to teacher training, and the in-service training of teachers, as instruments for handing over practical experience and for educational development and change.

In making these points we ought to record that many who have to work with the new arrangements feel the present balance of power to be about right and the system to be excellent. We do know, however, that there is a feeling among some that the two boards are too powerful and too insulated from political control. Our concern, however, is less with the nature of the power struggles at the centre than with the new alignment of forces where the work happens, namely at the school and institutional level. In this, we feel that vertical decentralisation has been vigorous but that the points we have made need attention. It is at the local level that so much development work is necessary. Horizontal participation between such institutions as schools and teacher training centres needs careful and patient work. Teacher training institutions have to put themselves into a service-giving and consultancy relationship with schools that, reciprocally, have to be eager to develop themselves. Participation within the schools can easily become ritualistic, so that teacher trade union representatives and a small minority of vocal and active pupils make the running. True pupil and teacher participation lies deep within the educational process when ideas are tested and modes of expression of them developed reciprocally between teacher and pupils. So devolution to the municipality, to the school and to the class are all necessary. These are matters of art and style as much as of machinery. Within the higher education system there is, too, a danger that representative figures are cut out of cardboard and that the ablest academics simply retreat into a private world or, like Plato's philosopher, shelter under the tree until the storm has passed. Care needs to be taken to determine how the social input to research and scholarship can be most fruitfully arranged. It may not be through the assertion of written representative rights. The behavioural consequences of making representative constitutions for institutions where individual work is so important have as yet not been thought through. Our hope is that different groups will learn to pull together to create not only good policies but good work.

In school decentralisation we perceive many different modes of participation jostling with each other. There remains the main line of participation through parliamentary and local elections which accord power and authority to the Parliament, the Ministry, the boards, the counties and the municipalities. It is from that traditional ballot box democracy that the professionals, the bureaucrats and the rectors derive their authority. Alongside these traditional routes of authority, corporatism gives representation through different groups which are not elected by the whole people but nonetheless have a genuine representative base. And then there is grass roots participation of those who are mainly and immediately affected by what happens in education, the professional practitioners and the clients. The scheme for decentralisation accepts that national prescription cannot work alone. But the decentralisation schemes do carry with them detailed prescriptions for the ways in which values and processes should be administered locally. The development of expression and style will have to come, however, from a different source, namely, the bottom rather than the top of the system.

VII

CONCLUSION

1. EDUCATION AND ITS SOCIAL FUNCTIONS

We came away from Sweden impressed, even overwhelmed, by the magnitude and results of the changes that had been effected. The degree of commitment that runs through the whole of the Swedish educational enterprise derives surely from the multiple participation that develops insight and a sense of responsibility in so many individuals and organisations. This relatively small country has earned its leadership role by the enormous input of thought, planning, feeling and resources of all kinds that it has committed to doing the best that it can for all its citizens. Sweden's disappointments and failures are, therefore, not those of intention, nor of lack of sophistication or skill. They are partly inherent in the nature of the attempts being made and partly caused by factors of a more general, social nature. We have already referred, in our introductory section, to those areas where Swedes themselves feel that success has not been fully achieved. Social and sex inequality in education has not been completely eliminated. Change is still at the level of overall structure rather than that of impact, practice and individual development and satisfaction. It has created a comprehensive all-through school system, and has virtually abolished geographical inequality. It has improved the educational level and opportunities of working class children and of girls. It has reformed higher education and provided excellent facilities for adult education. It has made decisive policies for the integration of the education of handicapped children. It has worked, with empathy and concern, to integrate, but yet respect, the particular needs of immigrants. It has built up research and development in all of its sectors. In all of these things it remains a leading example of educational reform. In all of these reforms, however, there remain problems and ambiguities which we state here as the basis for further discussion with the Swedish authorities at the Review meeting.

We recognise the skilful way in which Sweden has related structural changes in favour of equality to changes in the whole scope, and mode of working, of education in the schools and colleges. Our general conclusion is that whilst the need for individual and differential impact is fully recognised, it is unlikely to be achieved until the working style and ethos of the schools change so as to secure stronger individual professionalism among teachers in what they can regard as institutions where their own development and creativity have a full place. It is this balance between social engineering and individual development that as yet needs to be struck for the sake of equality and for other desirable objectives in Sweden.

2. THE ISSUE OF EQUALITY

The different stages of equality (opportunity, access, positive inducement to the underprivileged, and individualised impact) have been discussed in Chapter III of this report. Each stage seems to raise different obstacles to the achievement of equality and make different demands upon the education and social system generally. Present Swedish policies are still concerned with completing structural changes. However, we would raise three questions.

> First, is enough work being done on experimental educational modes which will produce methods that make possible a comprehensive and integrated structure? Second, how, within the curriculum, will Sweden reconcile the conflict of objectives between overall equality and the needs of individual development and refreshment? Third, is it not possible that some pupils would benefit from differentiation in length and speed of course before the end of the grundskola?

The grundskola secures access to nine years of compulsory education for all, and this is a great achievement in its own right. The provision for the comprehensive gymnasium is also impressive.

> We wonder, however, whether the schemes for following up school leavers, and other modes of reinforcing pupils' choices, will secure recruitment to the gymnasium of those most particularly in need of post-school education, namely, the less able and well off? For that matter, it might be asked whether the gymnasium really meets the needs of such young people.

The development of post-gymnasium provision is most impressive as regards both the adult and recurrent educational facilities and the restructuring of universities and colleges. We recognise that the latest rules for access (the 25/4 Rule) and the associated methods of selection have only just been introduced. Even those sympathetic to the objectives, however, are somewhat worried about what they see as the balance between criteria of teaching and research excellence and the need to cater for the groups newly recruited to higher education.

For example, will the numerus clausus and other restrictions on recruitment (such as the division of applicants into four groups) be kept under review to make sure that particular sections of the community are not penalised because of the Swedish authorities' determination to secure inter-generational equality?

3. EDUCATIONAL CONTENT AND METHODS

The Background Report directly identifies issues of teaching style, motivation and ethos. The extent to which teachers cease to rely upon existing patterns of authority and strengthen their own and pupils' learning and developmental motivation will be the key to making almost all of Sweden's educational reforms truly operative. Education needs to become more reflexive and interactive rather than prescriptive and academic. Whilst fully respecting the need to relate to the world outside, intellectual standards need to be maintained and advanced so that teaching, for pupils of all ability levels, induces competence in basic skills, but also a respect for evidence, for experiment, for the ability to form concepts and explore initiatives. We note the excellent initiatives in giving teachers five days a year in which in-service training may be given. We also note that teachers may visit other schools. The development of school-based in-service training, in which teachers themselves take initiatives and build up their own intellectual and professional networks, would be highly desirable.

4. THE SCHOOL AND ITS RELATIONSHIP TO PARENTS AND THE COMMUNITY

The relationship between the school and society is particularly important in the relationships between teachers and parents. We feel that as the municipalities acquire stronger control over the curriculum, the school should be emphasised as a unit at which curriculum development can take place. At that time, it should be possible for teachers to establish active and strong connections with groups of parents and other members of the community able to give assistance. The social values implicit in all education can thus be elucidated with all important client groups and curriculum development tested with them. This does not mean that teachers should or need capitulate to the sometimes inconsistent pressures from outside the school, but that they should take account of social demands as they formulate the curriculum in the light of the knowledge of their pupils' development, the concepts and data of the different subject areas, and other information which feeds into the curriculum. We have argued that the strongly integrated education system must put all the more emphasis on to individual differentiation. Thus, there are two models of change, sequential to each other. The first is to create national objectives and a system within which, eventually, decentralisation and democratisation will ensure that the individual school and teacher will have room for their own development within their community. In Sweden it is fair to say that most of the effort has gone into creating the system and that now, at a relatively late stage, when teachers and society as a whole accept national direction as the normal mode of working, attempts are being made to bring psychological release into the basic levels of education. The second model, following the first reform, is more oriented to interaction between pupils and teachers, to the classroom and the school as the prime institutions. But that second model, which is surely likely to be most conducive to teacher and pupil creativity, obviously creates problems of securing equality and other national policies. It leads us into more general problems of participation and policy creation. For the authorities the challenge is twofold:

- How to develop effective decentralisation and democratisation so as to increase the role of parents and the community in the work of the school? How to establish strong models of local participation, at the school and municipal level, and yet retain equality and reasonable uniformity of standards throughout the Swedish system?

5. LINKS WITH WORKING LIFE

The reforms attempt, through many devices, to strengthen links between education, work and life outside the school and the university. We applaud the scope and intention of these efforts but now raise potential problems and dangers. We have been told that there is a danger of anti-intellectualism in Sweden which is certainly not necessarily implicit in anything that we have seen in the Swedish authorities' plans but which might be deduced from some particular emphases within them. Thus, the emphasis on the world of work as against the implied academicism of universities, colleges and schools, might be a desirable change in emphasis. But the role of education is multiple. It must advance the causes of theory, concept-forming and science as well as those of social relevance and vocational skills.

Moreover, we are not clear that the labour and economic functions of education have been put in a realistic enough setting. Educational opportunities grow. So do individual expectations. We devoutly hope that the Swedes are right to assume that the economy will be able to sustain the good life for which pupils are being prepared in the schools; but, too often, expectations are increasingly incapable of being matched by the income, status and work that pupils will experience outside. Some pupils compare unfavourably the education they know with the world of work about which some may fantasise. Yet employment problems are acute for school leavers. It is important that education is seen as a value in itself. For this reason, we are slightly anxious about the emphasis on the relationship between education and the labour market. Even if all courses were made productively and economically relevant (and we must not exaggerate the tendency towards vocationalism) it is by no means clear that the economy could absorb all of these better qualified people. There could easily be a problem of perceived "over-skill"; there need never be a problem of over-education if education is seen in terms of its more general social and cultural advantages. Education is multi-purpose. It helps individuals to understand their predicaments even when they cannot always solve them. Solutions to the disequilibrium between labour demand and supply in an increasingly educated society lie outside the education field.

> What is clear is that further thought is required in the total government system about the relationship between labour supply from education, take-up, placement and reward within the labour market, and the expectations of pupils and parents, and the multiple functions of education. Moreover, it is necessary to strive for an adequate balance within the schools between an emphasis on the world of work and the experiences that they can bring to bear on the total educational process, as against the need for strong cognitive, social and other development.

6. CENTRAL GOVERNMENT AND ROLLING REFORM

Swedish education has moved from a fairly technocratic and consensual model of educational government to one in which politics are expected to be far more open and where decisions made by a closed elite, no matter how democratically appointed, are no longer so acceptable. The developing power of the municipalities, of individual teachers, of the teaching profession, of the unions, of parents, pupils and students will both complicate and contribute to the work of keeping reform rolling towards defined and stable objectives. We believe that these moves, although they might take Swedish institutions through periods of conflict and dissensus, are healthy. We believe that the encouragement to research and development given by the two national boards will contribute in a most positive way to the elaboration of choice of all who must participate in decisions. But we also feel that the independent intelligentsia should get to work on the Swedish system in addition to those who receive funds for decision-oriented research.

Traditional centralisation has given way to what could easily become equally institutionalised forms of participation. Within each municipality and its schools many forces can equally well come into conflict or into co-operation with each other. The school has to work with the constructs created by the national authorities, the municipalities, those working in the school - teachers and other workers - the trade unions, the parents and the pupils and the individual teachers. Within that complex, a choice will eventually have to be made by Swedish society as to where it is prepared to allow leadership to develop. Participation by parents in school means that teachers must be prepared to help parents analyse what they seek for their children in education. Teachers must then translate those expectations into influences on the curriculum. There is, we feel, a vacuum in thinking about how the dynamics of power and development at the local level will be better encouraged, articulated and dissolved into co-operative working.

7. HIGHER EDUCATION

Similar issues arise in higher education. Decentralisation to the education units for the working out of curriculum and resource allocation is admirable in principle. The system of regional co-ordination throughout the six boards of education certainly needs a longer period for fair testing: they will either prove themselves to be a redundant addition of another level of administration, or will earn their way in terms of influencing the higher education structure in favour of the wider range of activities considered for higher education. Our concern lies in other directions. We could get no clear picture of what Swedish society wants and expects of its higher education teachers and researchers. In higher education more than anywhere else, good work depends upon individual motivation and creativity. Those qualities need not be incompatible with respect for relevance to society (that being a concept developed by academics themselves) or the social need of students and of the economy and of society at large. But we have to record a certain degree of demoralisation in higher education about the status of teaching and research. In their attempt to broaden access, the Swedish authorities have accorded new status and created new organisations for much higher education that so far has had no research component and where the standards must be extremely variable. At the same time, established institutions are coping with far older students, many of whom do not have the same high level of academic qualifications as younger undergraduates. The division between teaching and research which is about to be bridged adds to the problems of retaining in universities a sense that academic work should be an exciting but many-faceted venture, in which good balance is encouraged between the education of the next generation, the collation of knowledge, and its analysis through scholarship and the generation of knowledge through research and development. Social objectives of education have been well promulgated in Sweden.

The problems that we have outlined here could arise only in a country where so much effort has been expended and so much achieved. The problems facing the Swedes face many countries. There is hardly any precept of human advancement that is not ambiguous. The two main touchstones of Swedish reform have been equality and, then, participation. But both of these words mean so many different things. Equality of opportunity, of access and of take-up are all different stages of advance. And equality of what is provided and what is taken up does not mean equality of impact and reception by the individual. People start from and finish up at different places. These facts of life mock and challenge the best intentions of social reformers. How can one plan for individual wants and diversities and at the same time be fair, and create a viable, productive society? Participation, too, has for so long meant participation through the electoral process. But now it means participation through elections and political activity, participation through non-governmental institutions such as trade unions and other associations accepted as having automatic corporate rights and, more recently, participation as a client, or a student or as a pupil or as a professor, researcher or other practitioner who has a right to join in and help formulate the way in which services are created and delivered. And yet if participation means so many things, it also produces precisely the same problems as do the multiple concepts of equality. For if all can participate in so many ways, a system still has to exist which holds things together so as to avoid inequality, inefficiency, disjunction between desirably connected values and objectives, and accountability of institutions to the wider public and nation. The problem facing Sweden is not that of commitment and intention. Nor is it, thanks to Sweden's qualities as a productive and serious society, a problem primarily of resources, even as they have more carefully to count the cost of what they want to do. It is rather one of flexibility. Because if ambiguity mocks the planner, it is also an expression of the richness of life and of the educational experiences which schools and colleges can offer pupils. Making a constructive use of ambiguity is thus the challenge which Sweden faces. Can so committed a society tolerate and work with all of the uncertainties which its own successes have generated? Can uncertainty be the fertile soil for new ideas and new practice, for alternatives rather than fixed positions?

Part Two

RECORD OF THE REVIEW MEETING
(Paris, 13th November 1979)

I

EDUCATION AND ITS SOCIAL FUNCTION
AND THE ISSUE OF EQUALITY

Mr. Arfwedson began by explaining the most recent changes in policies for the comprehensive school, these being changes which had not been fully apparent at the time of the examiners' visit. Following the 1976 reforms, there had been debate about how to improve the prospects for the most disadvantaged, not simply by giving them equal treatment but by ensuring that there would be greater equality of outcomes. But although the general intention had been expressed in 1976 it was discovered that once political intentions were converted into curriculum proposals different interpretations arose. The earlier measures had proposed the abolition of options in the upper forms of secondary school so as to equalise opportunities. The National Board of Education had been in favour of the abolition of options. After a lively debate, however, Parliament had reached the conclusion that the traditional approach of abolishing options would not induce more equal chances for the less advantaged children and that, therefore, the alternative, i.e. more options, should be adopted. The Ministry of Education had accordingly revised the proposals put up by the National Board. This policy touched on one of the questions posed by the examiners, namely: "How, within the curriculum, will Sweden reconcile the conflict of objectives between overall equality and the needs of individual development and refreshment?".

Mr. Johansson said that the Swedish interpretation of school reform was that equality required a varied curriculum to enable different approaches to be made to the same subject. It was essential, however, that different options should not restrict the pupils' possible alternatives in further studies. It also involved changed relationships between teachers, for example team-teaching, and between teachers and pupils, so that there would be a true exercise of choice. They were concerned as well, however, that there should be a balance between good basic knowledge and skills and the development of individual interests and talents. There had been serious attempts to encourage a pupil-centred approach in education but they had not succeeded. The detailed proposals included a requirement that local authorities, which would be responsible for the optional part of the curriculum, should make sure that each school offered periods for free activity.

The Swedish government was allocating extra funds to help assure the pupils' acquisition of basic writing, speech, reading and arithmetic skills by means of small group instruction. The proposal also stressed the need for factual knowledge. The importance of homework was to be emphasised. About one-third of the time at senior level would be devoted to studies of the pupils' own choice and school activities would be decided locally. The free choices of studies would comprise optional subjects, free activities, which would form a bridge between school work and the pupils' leisure activities for two periods a week in each of the classes 7, 8 and 9, and in-depth studies for about four periods a week in each class. The optional subject courses and content would mainly be decided locally but all schools would be bound to offer optional courses in French and German (in addition to compulsory English). Immigrant pupils would be able to choose the study of their native language as an optional subject. In the gymnasium there would be changes, particularly in the language programme, so as to give pupils a more profound knowledge of languages. An advanced course of English or maths would no longer be required as a condition for admission to the three- or four-year lines in the gymnasium. Other proposals would aim at breaking down the traditional sex role pattern so as to promote greater equality between boys and girls. New working methods which would emphasise alternance between the practical and exploratory, on the one hand, and theory and explanation, on the other, would be introduced. Marks would be retained in the comprehensive school but only in grades 8 and 9. The relation between school and working life would be vigorously built up.

These changes would be carried out within a framework of increased local responsibility. Individual schools would be responsible for the content of their teaching and there would be more freedom to allocate money and resources to best advantage. Pupils would have more power to influence the school environment. A local plan of work for school activities would be drawn up in each school management area, which would incorporate the choice of study and associated programmes. The new curriculum would be introduced from the academic year 1982-83. Local implementation grants would be made available so as to allow teachers to plan and prepare for the new curriculum. County education boards would receive funds to expand their information, planning and development activities.

Mr. Arfwedson added that these proposals would open up new opportunities for local authorities and the schools themselves. Moreover, the answer to the first question put by the examiners was that experimental work on a large scale would be undertaken.

Mrs. Eide asked whether adults other than teachers would take part in the life of the school. If so, there were dangers to be foreseen. For example, the parents who participated might be unrepresentative of the parents at large and exert an influence leading away from and not towards equality. Mr. van Kemenade added that there was also a danger of accentuating inequality through the addition of options whereas greater choice within a uniform framework could ensure differentiation without importing inequality. The Swedish Delegation replied that the most important aspect of the proposed changes was the emphasis on individual study and treatment. This was reckoned to be more important than the structure of options provided. Moreover, all pupils would be following a strong basic foundation course. Differentiation, through the use of options and through individual instruction, would be additional to that. Mr. Arfwedson stressed that more time would be allowed to teachers for reflection and preparation. At the same time, teachers were not expected to see their professional role simply as a function of the number of hours spent in the classroom.

On the question of parents, he said that up to now the main problem had been how to get them interested at all in participating in school life. There was no tradition of parental participation in schools and it would not be easy to secure their participation on a large scale. It would be starting at the wrong end, therefore, to worry about whether the participation was representative or not, when it might not be happening at all.

Mr. Kogan said that the controversy about options within the curriculum was a good example of the difficulty of defining advances in the latest stage of equality, namely, that of ensuring individual impact. Securing the final stage of equality involved quite hard technical and detailed work on procedures. Not everyone would be convinced that individualised impact would be secured if some optional system were not allowed. Moreover, the account given of curriculum changes demonstrated how difficult it was for even a strongly committed national system to secure changes at the working level without corresponding change in the individuals within the teaching profession.

UPPER SECONDARY EDUCATION

The discussion then turned to the upper secondary schools. Mr. Orehag said that the gymnasium had brought together several different lines lasting two, three or four years. Some were theoretical and a preparation for further academic work, while others were preparations for the world of work. Flexible arrangements enabled different aspirations to be met. The gymnasium was also attempting to strengthen the connections between education and the labour market, with which co-operation was being strongly developed. In all there were 22 or 23 lines that could be followed.

Mrs. Eide said that the new gymnasium structure was among the most imaginative innovations for securing good opportunities for young people. There still remained the question, however, as to whether all young people should be remaining in full-time education. This obliged the schools to adapt to underlying needs which might well be better catered for elsewhere. Mr. Ekholm replied that this was precisely the reason why a new kind of gymnasium, deliberately structured not to create a strong dividing line between school and working life, had been devised. The National Commission on the Gymnasium had not yet reported but it was clear that the gymnasium was also helping to meet some of the problems caused by youth unemployment. The state grant system would enable local school authorities to strengthen the range of subjects offered by the gymnasium. They would probably have, to a higher degree than today, the responsibility for planning and surveying needs.

ADMISSION TO HIGHER EDUCATION

Mr. Ekholm described the 25/4 Rule to which reference had been made on page 76 of the Examiners' Report. He explained that there were dual requirements for admission to higher education. All candidates had to meet the special requirements, which included knowledge in certain subjects corresponding to two- or three-year courses within the gymnasium as appropriate for the particular course about to be pursued. The general requirement was successful completion of a gymnasium course or comparable working experience within the 25/4 Rule. There had been a change towards recruiting students who were older on average.

Other important changes concerned the very concept of higher education. For example, nursing and other paramedical activities had traditionally had separate training systems. Now they were becoming regarded as part of the legitimate range of higher education, and were all now part of the same system. Mr. Ringborg then explained the position on numerus clausus. Changes in the average age of the freshmen had already been occurring before the revision of the selection rules. The numbers who went directly to university from school had already diminished as a proportion. It had been thought necessary to give possibilities to restrict the entry even to courses that had traditionally free access so as to get a planning situation where it was possible to weigh different needs and interests of higher education against each other within the resource frames given. All the same, it was recognised that for some time to come the selection rules needed to be kept under review, and that was being done.

It was certainly not intended to penalise certain groups, as the examiners had implied. Nevertheless, it was recognised that where competition was fierce, pupils who might have previously expected to gain admission to a course straight from school on the strength of their gymnasium record might now find that they would have first to spend some time in a paid occupation.

PRE-SCHOOL EDUCATION AND HELP TO THE DISADVANTAGED

There was some discussion of the importance of co-operation between the different authorities for health, education and welfare in taking care of the needs of pre-school children. Proposals for joint training had been made. It was possible for children coming from disadvantaged social groups as well as children with mental and physical handicaps to enter nursery classes earlier than others.

Mr. van Kemenade asked why the Swedes hesitated to have special education programmes for the children of poor families. There were no explicit compensatory programmes for disadvantaged neighbourhoods. Was this because of a fear of stigmatising families or did the Swedish authorities feel that such programmes would not be effective? Mr. Arfwedson replied that disadvantaged children were to be found everywhere, especially in the major urban areas, but there were no large concentrations of them. The new system of grants to local schools permitted resources to be used for differential treatment. The size of these grants was based on both the number of pupils enrolled and on a needs element. It was not yet clear, however, how local authorities were using their funds, but inquiries were under way. The Canadian Delegate asked whether it would be sufficient simply to put extra money into the less favoured environments. The key requirement must be greater participation of parents and measures to secure the most direct way of helping disadvantaged pupils. Was it feasible to pass legislation requiring parental participation? The Swedish authorities had apparently decided to proceed along lines other than those followed by the United States authorities where success, too, had been uncertain. The Swedish Delegation replied that school districts might be uniform but schools were by no means all alike; for example, some schools contained sizeable numbers of children from minority ethnic groups. Schools were not sure to make appropriate responses to the needs of their clientele simply because extra funds were available and this was why the Swedish government laid so much emphasis upon individualisation of method and the growth of individual patterns of work. This was also why attempts were being made to intensify parental participation in the activities of the schools.

The Norwegian Delegate remarked that the discussion revealed different attitudes towards the way education might be provided.

The Swedish government seemed concerned to demonstrate their ability to produce a "cafeteria" for education whilst the examiners seemed to be arguing for different forms of intermediate theory. He asked whether the Swedish government intended to abolish the use of marks. Such educational decisions directly influenced what was being done to promote equality. The problem of educational participation was deep rooted. In Norway, participation in higher education ranged between 15 per cent and 50 per cent according to social class and the lower levels of participation remained among the lower social groups. Had the final proportions been reached in either country? Ultimately, the phenomenon which had to be reckoned with was the ability of specialist and professional groups to maintain a hold over education when it should be more susceptible to the influence of wider social and client groups. The Swedish Delegation replied that marks had been abolished in grades 1 to 7 and remained only in 8 and 9. This was the result of a political compromise. But they were to be used differently. There were to be experimental admissions to the gymnasium without the use of marks. The issue of marks was, however, becoming a deeply difficult and complicated one. It was not yet clear which criteria should be used to judge the success of pupils at school. There was then the issue of what system could be used to avoid selection processes. Both of these issues were tied up with the drive towards decentralisation. A local school authority needed power to change the way in which it delivered the curriculum as students began to develop their own views about what should be the main local emphasis. At the same time there was the conflicting need to control entry to oversubscribed higher education lines. Several other criteria needed to be taken into account. There was the point in a career when applicants attempted to enter higher education. There was the work experience demonstrated by candidates and the need, as well, to secure an adequate sex balance. Some of these questions might be resolved by planning but others might have to be answered by the use of a lottery.

The New Zealand Delegate raised questions about the use of marks and the marking system which linked with the issue of social mobility. The questioning of the marking system might not be sufficiently fundamental. The logic of the Gaussian Curve which always made for set distributions seemed still to dominate. Were there no alternative ways of responding to the changing pattern of student and parental wishes? The Swedish Delegation replied that they had moved away from dependence on the Gaussian Curve although still grading on a scale of 0 to 5. In any event, pupils in grades 1 to 7 were not subjected to a marking scheme but judgements were formed and discussed in meetings between parents and teachers. Aptitude tests were used simply as tests of the whole group of students. Other delegations raised particular points relevant to the discussion. Interest was expressed in the extent to which the common courses had really moved. Were they still traditional in content and method? (Netherlands). Was there a combination of aptitude tests with other forms of test? (Yugoslavia) The Swedish Delegation replied that there was no combination. Research was continuing into the use made of aptitude tests and their efficacy.

The Finnish Delegate asked what happened to the 25 per cent of those who did not go to the gymnasium. What was the composition of the 25 per cent and were they heavily orientated towards the migrant groups? The Swedish Delegation replied that only 10 per cent left education for good. Fifteen per cent came back later on to upper secondary school or higher education. There was undoubtedly too high a proportion of immigrants in the group that left.

The Danish Delegate asked what would happen with the introduction of the new curriculum for the grundskola. There was to be freedom for local authorities, teachers and the school. But what about the traditionalist teachers who insist on adhering to prescriptions? Similarly, with regard to the reform of upper secondary education, what would happen to schools allergic to change? The Swedish authorities were attempting to produce educational patterns which relied on sensitive evaluative modes rather than on the Gaussian Curve, which implied distrust of the schools. The Irish Delegate added that the issue of differentiation must remain. Was it possible to deal with students who experienced learning difficulties without stigmatising them?

The German Delegate asked what was the philosophy behind creating short courses of ten weeks in the upper end of the secondary school. Was it to introduce the students to working life or was it to broaden their general educational background? He also asked what was the quantitative importance of the numerus clausus. What percentage failed to enter higher education as a result of it? Did the different forms of upper secondary education create the same eligibility for higher education? Mr. Papadopoulos (OECD Secretariat) asked whether there was any change in the social background of those entering the different lines in higher education. Mr. Arfwedson answered that the effects of the numerus clausus were not yet clear. The pattern certainly varied according to the subjects studied. Students had become older on entry because of the weighting given to work experience: most students had first spent some time, be it long or short, in the labour market - in Medicine, for example, the average age of admission was 25-30 years, and a cause for some dissent. Almost all students in the three types of lines in upper secondary education (theoretical, vocational or mixed theoretical and vocational) were entitled to apply for admission to higher education. But they were also all required to meet the special requirements stated earlier at the meeting. About 15 to 20 per cent entering higher education came from the vocational lines and there was a hopeful tendency for an increase in

91

those taking the two-year gymnasium course to enter higher education. The proportion was, however, as yet quite small. But at least the channels to higher education had been opened up. The social class differentiation among entrants was now the subject of research, e.g. in terms of four different age cohorts. Current evidence showed that social differentiation persisted. The most gifted among working-class children had now the same chances to enter higher education as those in other social classes. On an average, however, their chances were much smaller than those of equally able children in other social classes. But the integration of the technical and vocational lines into the gymnasium undoubtedly increased the chances of equality.

II

EDUCATIONAL CONTENT AND METHODS

Mr. van Kemenade said that questions about content and methods brought one to the heart of the matter. There were two central dilemmas. The first was how to reconcile collective goals with individual impact. The second was how to reconcile the universalistic criteria of the market with social values. Hitherto there had been solutions for these dilemmas but they had been elitist and they had now given way to more democratic and egalitarian modes. Comprehensive schools might reduce elitism between schools but there were dangers of a new meritocracy being developed within them through the opportunities they gave to working-class children. These problems were intimately concerned with the development of the curriculum and the more important difference must be to handle the individual requirements of pupils through the same curriculum. Mr. Johansson replied that the intended reforms would be implemented in four ways. There was first the question of how school itself would work. Here the SIA reforms, notably reforms of the working life of the school, were relevant. Schools would be broken down into smaller work units to enable them to be more responsive to individual needs. Head teachers would be helped to initiate the new developments through four-week leadership courses and other measures. Teachers, recreational workers, welfare officers and others would be given special training and formed into teams of 15 for each district so that a school could develop to its full potential. All schools must prepare a work plan. And, finally, there was the new curriculum which had already been discussed at the meeting. The districts would receive implementation grants, so that the schools would find it easier to meet the requirement to provide options. Some 40 million Swedish Kronor a year or a total of 180 million Swedish Kronor would be given for this purpose and this was the largest grant ever awarded for educational development. Teachers could be released for special training so as to enhance their skills in handling special educational programmes.

It could not be assumed that all pupils would reach equal levels but it could certainly be insisted that all should reach the highest level of which they were capable. This would not be achieved through ability grouping. Schools would pay attention to the hidden curriculum and there would be a redevelopment of team teaching within work units so that the maximum range of offerings could be developed collectively. The work units would seek to ensure that the general core of the curriculum was developed as a flexible instrument. Mrs. Eide asked whether these new opportunities would be positively welcomed by teachers. Mr. Arfwedson replied that the teachers' unions were negotiating on the provisions and that there was some difference of opinion between central and local unions over the resulting impact on distribution of the teacher's working day. Generally, however, teachers had been accustomed to receiving orders from above; all the major reforms until 1970 had been prescriptive in tone. The 1976 SIA proposals had attempted to move that prescriptive flavour from Swedish education.

Mr. van Kemenade asked whether there was room for the development of free schools in Sweden. Were such experimental practices as those of the Montessori and Freinet schools permissible? Mr. Arfwedson replied that there had been little development of this kind although it was hoped that particularly in early schooling more experiments would occur.

The Swiss Delegate asked whether teachers would be able to control an educational pattern that seemed to be so tailor-made. Had teachers' unions and individual teachers been consulted on this reform? Was it possible to have a curriculum that was both "globalised" and yet capable of meeting the needs of individual pupils? Could schools go beyond the possibilities implied by the curriculum as laid down? Mr. Johansson replied that all schools had had a full day for discussion of the proposals. The teachers' unions were fully consulted on its provisions and the Bill itself was subject to a full consultative process. In Parliament, teachers' unions were brought in for discussion at committee stage. On the educational content of the reforms, the system of work units would make it possible for there to be different sizes of classes and varying groups for different purposes although grouping on ability would be avoided. Ability grouping for more than one term would only be permitted after consultation with the pupils. The Belgian Delegate questioned the extent to which it was possible for individuals to reach their own level when a common core was enforced. On the face of it this seemed to be a contradiction in terms. Mr. van Kemenade remarked that whilst a common core would certainly involve equal measures, the later stages of education in no sense implied equal handling.

The New Zealand Delegate said that whilst the Swedish Background Report in Chapter 5 implied that the criteria of success must be multiple, Chapter 4 was disappointingly dependent on the International Association for the Evaluation of Educational Achievement (IEA) surveys. There was nothing to indicate whether standards had changed over time but only a snapshot of standards given on somewhat narrow criteria, because the IEA tests measure only some of the outcomes of schooling and the criteria were almost wholly cognitive. The Swedish Delegation agreed that the criteria were narrow but said there was general acceptance that the level of achievement on the whole was not good enough whether or not it had now improved. Mr. Kogan wondered whether in moving towards new systems with new criteria some loss might have to be accepted, at least during the period of transition.

Mrs. Eide said that in bringing hitherto separate forms of higher education within the traditional academic framework the concept of equality might be distorted. On the face of it, hitherto low status higher education might thereby enhance its standing. But, equally, it might be compelled to shed its socially estimable values in order to conform with the traditional norms of higher education.

III

THE SCHOOL AND ITS RELATIONSHIP TO PARENTS AND THE COMMUNITY

Mrs. Eide believed that this part of the discussion should be carried out against the background of what had already been considered in terms of the curriculum and particularly the SIA reforms. The central issue was what role should be given to the parent in relationship to the development of the school and the stage of education reached. It was possible to think of the community as a learning environment, a kind of external laboratory in which the school could develop. Alternatively, the community could be an entity to which schools conformed and which was part of the socialising environment of education. Again, it was possible to think of the community as being inimical to the school. In this case the school might become an agent for changing society and schools increasingly might be seen as taking what some would regard as intolerable political actions concerned, for example, with ecological issues or issues of participation or issues of general politics. Did the Swedish authorities consider the school within any or all of these contexts? If so, there might be conflict with formal notions of the aims of the schools. The Swedish Delegation replied that some of these normative questions were now being studied by a commission. At present it was obvious that the school was not making clear connections with the community and it was not possible to know what were the true relationships between the school and the community. The Swedish authorities hoped that all of these concepts of the community and the school could be handled simultaneously and certainly Swedish developments in the modes of **partici**pation and co-determination, as well as of the more strictly educational reforms, pointed in the direction of a multi-form school relating closely to the community. In these respects, however, Sweden should not only be a model but also part of a warning system. It was not easy to deal with these many changes in values all at once. For one thing, such issues as co-determination and the developing role of the school board were affected by the belief of some that the trade unions had too strong a position whilst the individual teacher remained too weak. Nonetheless, it was clear that teachers were in favour of the parents coming in. Mrs. Eide observed that it might well be that there should be reform of labour law so that each parent could be released from work for at least one day a year to go and spend time in his or her children's school.

IV

HIGHER EDUCATION

Mrs. Eide stated that the Examiners' Report had not said a great deal about higher education but the importance of what was being done in this sector was enormous. The system was being carefully monitored by the Swedish authorities and this was just as well because expectations were being raised throughout the whole country. Some of the criticisms that the examiners had noted took the form of an anti-intellectualism which could too easily be associated with reforms that were necessary and right in their own terms. Mr. Ringborg replied that the period of preparation for reform had taken far too long and during this period a lot of circumstances independent of the reform had undoubtedly contributed towards the "demoralisation" within higher education of which the examiners had written. Because of the delay in introducing change those affected naturally blamed the institutional arrangements themselves. As a matter of fact, reform was coinciding with a period that would have been demoralising anyway because the period of expansion had to come to an end. A much needed reform was still that of improving the structure of careers for teachers and researchers. Far more flexibility was needed to allow each department to be more free within the new framework. The system had thus changed but the major benefits of it to individuals and small groups were not as yet felt.

Mr. van Kemenade said that many measures had been instituted all at once. There was the associated problem of the management of research. Research was being determined at a committee level rather than through individuals or an agreed system. Mr. Kogan added that higher education was a prime example of the way in which reform had inevitably to be stated at the systemic and institutional level but there the criteria variables must be individual. A potential criticism of the Swedish reforms was that those variables were not borne in mind and sufficiently monitored as systemic change was introduced. Mr. Ringborg replied that important changes in teaching methods would result from more representative social groups coming into higher education as well as changes in the administrative structures. Curriculum was being adapted within the institutions and it was hoped there would be a good adjustment between scholarship and the wider needs which higher education should meet. The distribution between younger and older students might mean that there were changes in the way in which the higher education staff worked which certainly could have an effect. It was too early to say, however, what would be the impact of the changes on the recruitment for research work about which some anxiety had been expressed. It was also clear that local university boards had not delegated power within the institutions in the way that they could have done.

The Norwegian Delegate pointed out that there was a binary system in Norway and a unitary one in Sweden. On the face of it this implied that a strong national system was supporting a monopoly in higher education. Should a single professional group have so much power? Mr. Ekholm replied to these points that there was a determined effort to broaden the whole scope of higher education. The formerly subordinate professions such as nursing were now being brought into the higher education system. Chairs were being set up in social work. Links with research were being forged. No damage had been inflicted on existing research facilities. Research councils were able to allocate funds in the same way as before the reforms.

V

CENTRAL GOVERNMENT AND ROLLING REFORM

Mr. Kogan, referring to the role of the centre (page 72) asked what would be the effects of decentralisation on the role of the central authority. Could it take on a more strongly educative role in which prescriptive authority became reduced while leadership power became enhanced? Would the monitoring and dissemination of change become positive aspects of the centre's work? Might there not be a danger of a power vacuum as groups within the decentralised system found their place? Might not new rigidities develop whilst, at the same time, the centre became uncertain of its rights to intervene? Mr. Arfwedson wished to stress that the decentralisation move had perhaps been overstated. The central authorities would continue to handle the resource framework within which local authorities in both schools and higher education would act. They had powerful means for controlling higher education and the schools. It was not expected that there would be great regional variety, at least in the earlier stages. Another question which needed to be watched was whether equality might be reduced as different units throughout the country gained power following the relinquishment of central authority. But it was thought by the Swedish authorities that the freedom to be unequal would be restricted because of the resource frameworks.

VI

LINKS WITH WORKING LIFE

Mrs. Eide asked whether there was not a danger of assuming that placing practical courses within universities was not over-academicising learning opportunities that might be better placed elsewhere. There were different knowledge traditions which could too easily be homogenised within an artificial academic setting. Might there not be better environments outside higher education and the schools in which educative and training work could develop? Mr. van Kemenade added another dimension to the problem. There was an obvious concern about the relationship between education and the labour market, but structural unemployment and the general complexity of labour market conditions might make this linkage unacceptable to pupils who would be frustrated on leaving education. The Swedish Delegation replied that a wrong impression might have been given of the Swedish reforms. Employers and other groups within the world of work were closely connected with the changes in the curriculum and in the government of institutions. The Swedish authorities were not in favour of strict manpower planning. The Austrian Delegate remarked that the Swedish schemes gave a good lead on ways of identifying forms of continuing education and of relocating education from the school to the workplace. Mr. Arfwedson stated that it was not always desirable to bring vocational training into upper secondary education. Some forms of training were better carried out in enterprises and some young people wanted to get clear away from an educational environment at the end of compulsory schooling. In answer to a question from the Italian Delegate he added that his authorities were encouraging the development of recurrent education in higher education and actively considering its implications for upper secondary education.

VII

CONCLUDING REMARKS

Mr. van Kemenade said that almost all OECD Member countries faced the same problems. All were interested in Sweden's establishment of the comprehensive school but aware that structural integration was not sufficient either to establish true equality of opportunity or integration between education and working life. It was imperative to follow through by developing the curriculum and giving teachers the opportunity to deepen their understanding and ability to respond to the challenge of new assumptions. In achieving reform the importance of enabling the different groups to participate could not be under-estimated. The Examiners' Report had not perhaps sufficiently discussed the innovative power of participation by the pupils themselves. All countries were now at different stages of development but the 1980s were bound to be a turning point in education everywhere. Education for participation was all the more necessary as technical development changed the role of the individual within work and within society. The autonomous province of education would thus become reduced and at the same time there would be a power distribution in educational decision-making which needed careful adjustment and reflection.

Mr. Artwedson on behalf of the Swedish Delegation said that the Swedish authorities were fully conscious that there must be a lag between ambitions and actuality and it was upon removing this lag that they were working. They accepted that social engineering was insufficient in itself and that it was vitally important to ensure the involvement and support of everybody concerned with change. But they believed that support and commitment would find their natural place in the new reformed structure.

Annex

LIST OF MAIN SOURCES CONSULTED

OECD PUBLICATIONS AND DOCUMENTS

- Educational Policy and Planning, Sweden, 1967.

- Reviews of National Policies for Education, Sweden, 1969.

- Economic Surveys, Sweden, 1979.

- "Regional Effects of Swedish Educational Planning", by B. Hammarberg, F. Hedqvist, E. Holm, N. Haggström and N. Sundberg, in Education and Regional Development, Vol. II, Technical Reports, 1979.

- Innovation in In-Service Education and Training of Teachers, Sweden, CERI, 1976.

- "Developments in Recurrent Education: Sweden", 1977.

- Learning Opportunities for Adults, Vol. V, Widening Access to the Disadvantaged: A Swedish Case Study, forthcoming.

- New Patterns of Teacher Education and Tasks, Sweden, 1974.

- "Early Childhood Day Care in Sweden", by K. Sjöblom and K. Edenhammer, CERI, 1978 (mimeographed).

- The Evaluation of INSET for Teachers in Sweden, H. Eklund, CERI, 1978.

SWEDISH GOVERNMENT PUBLICATIONS
NATIONAL BOARD OF EDUCATION, INFORMATION SECTION BULLETINS

1(36)	Home Language Training, Home Language Teaching and Auxiliary Swedish Lessons in Pre-School, Compulsory School and Upper Secondary School
1(43)	Pupils with a Home Language other than Swedish or with a Non-Swedish Cultural Background
1976/04/12	Chief Education Officers, School Management and Teaching Staff in Swedish Compulsory Comprehensive Schools and Integrated Upper Secondary Schools: Their Responsibilities, Teaching Duties and Remuneration
1976/11/02:1(9) 1976/11/24:1(6)	The Integrated Upper Secondary School in Sweden
1977/08/29:1(22)	Adult Education on the Threshold of the 1980s - Some Guidelines for the work of the NBD.

103

1978/05/17 The Impact of Immigration on the Education System - A
            Draft Action Programme

Ministry of Economic Affairs and Ministry of the Budget, The Swedish Budget, 1979-80, 1979.

Ministry of Education and Cultural Affairs, Government Bill on the Working Conditions in Swedish Schools, 1976.

Ministry of Education and Cultural Affairs, The Reform of Higher Education, Government Bill, 1976-77.

National Board of Universities and Colleges, Higher Education for Immigrants and Political Refugees, 1978.

National Federation of Home and School Associations, A Contribution to the Current Debate on the SIA School, April 1978.

National Board of Education, Labour Market Training, 1975.

National Board of Education, Education Section, 1978/08/31, Costs.

Swedish Institute, Adult Education in Sweden, Fact Sheets on Sweden, 1978.

Swedish Trade Union Confederation, Education - Preparing for Work and Democracy, 1976.

National Board of Universities and Colleges, R & D for Higher Education, Information on Research and Development in Higher Education (several Bulletins).

National Board of Education, Educational Research and Development, 1976. A summary compiled by B. Estmer.

H. Bohlin, Co-determination in Decision-Making, University of Uppsala, 1979.

M. Bøye-Moller, "Language Training for Immigrant Workers in Sweden", International Labour Review, Vol. 108, No. 6, December, 1973.

E. Dahlström, Interaction between Practitioners and Social Scientists in Research and Development, National Board of Universities and Colleges, Dalaro, 1978.

C.T. Edam, The School in its Relation with the Community, National Board of Education, Information Section, CME/X(77), Conf/1.

M. Ekholm, School Age Education in Sweden, Reports Nos. 1 and 2, 1978.

B. Grünewald, Views of Swedish Industry on the Role of Public Education Swedish Employers' Confederation, 1979.

F. Halden, Problematics of Employment and Adaptation in Education, Training and Employment, Swedish Employers' Confederation, 1978.

J. Holbert, "The Parent-Teacher Movement in Sweden", Current Sweden, No. 128, August 1976.

L. Kim, "Widened Admission to Higher Education in Sweden (The 25/5 Scheme)" to be published in European Journal of Education.

U.P. Landgren and S. Pettersson, Code, Context and Curriculum Processes, Stockholm Institute of Education, Department of Educational Research, 1979.

J. Löfgren, Evaluation of Experimental Technical-Vocational College Courses, University of Lancaster, Fourth International Conference on Higher Education, 1978.

R.I.T. Premfors, The Politics of Higher Education in Sweden: Recent Developments (1976/78), Institution for Social and Policy Studies, Higher Education Research Group, Working Paper No. 30.

G. Rehn, Education and Youth Employment in Sweden (extract of forthcoming publication) (and table of social indices from part of same work).

O. Ruin, Educational Control and Participation, Trends in the Politics and Policies of Swedish Higher Education.

International Association for the Evaluation of Educational Achievement, 1978.

H. Östlund, "Strategic Planning on a Recurrent Basis", World Yearbook of Education, 1979.

T. Husén, "Educational Research and Educational Reform: A Case Study of Sweden" in B. Suppes, Impact of Research on Education, National Academy of Education, 1978.

ALREADY PUBLISHED

AUSTRALIA. TRANSITION FROM SCHOOL TO WORK OR FUTHER STUDY (November 1977)
(91 77 07 1) ISBN 92-64-12699-2, 110 pp. .... US$ 6.75   £3.30   F27,00   DM14.00   Can. $ 8.10

AUSTRIA (November 1970)
(91 70 01) 54 pp. .... Out of print

AUSTRIA. HIGHER EDUCATION AND RESEARCH (November 1976)
(91 76 08 1) ISBN 92-64-11555-2, 120 pp. .... US$ 5.50   £2.60   F22,00   DM11.00   Can. $ 6.60

AUSTRIA. SCHOOL POLICY (February 1979)
(91 79 01 1) ISBN 92-64-11891-8, 106 pp. .... US$ 6.00   £3.00   F24.00   DM12.00   Can. $ 7.20

CANADA (August 1976)
(91 76 06 1) ISBN 92-64-11545-5, 264 pp. .... US$ 9.00   £4.00   F36,00   DM18.00   Can. $10.80

DENMARK (June 1980)
(91 80 03 1) ISBN 92-64-12071-8, 162 pp. .... US$10.00   £4.70   F.42.00 DM21.00   Can. $12.60

FRANCE (February 1971)
(91 71 01 1) 166 pp. .... US$ 4.50   £1.50   F20,00   DM10.00   Can. $ 5.40

ENGLAND AND WALES (November 1975)
(91 75 03 1) ISBN 92-64-11347-9, 64 pp. .... Out of print

GERMANY (January 1973)
(91 72 08 1), 152 pp. .... Out of print

  German translation:
  BILDUNGSWESEN: MANGELHAFT, BRD-BILDUNGSPOLITIK IM OECD-LÄNDEREXAMEN
  Verlag Moritz Diesterweg,
  Hochstrasse 31, 6 Frankfurt/Main 1, Germany (F.R.)

IRELAND (February 1970)
(91 69 01 1) 142 pp. .... Out of print

ITALY (May 1969)
(91 69 02 1) 280 pp. .... Out of print

JAPAN (November 1971)
(91 71 06 1) 164 pp. .... Out of print

  Japanese translation available from Publications Department,
  The Asahi Shimbun, Tokyo, Japan.

NETHERLANDS (January 1971)
(91 69 06 1) 78 pp. .... Out of print

NETHERLANDS. CONTOURS OF A FUTURE EDUCATION STSTEM (September 1976)
(91 76 07 1) ISBN 92-64-11552-8, 94 pp.   .... US$ 4.00   £1.80   F16,00   DM 8.00   Can. $ 4.80

NORWAY (March 1970)
(91 76 02 1) ISBN 92-64-11481-5, 220 pp. .... Out of print

SWEDEN (July 1970)
(91 69 03 1) 70 pp. .... Out of print

UNITED STATES (November 1971)
(91 71 04 1), 434 pp. .... US$10.00   £3.45   F45,00   DM23.00   Can. $12.00

EDUCATION POLICIES IN PERSPECTIVE: AN APPRAISAL (Kogan, M.) (December 1979)
(91 79 08 1) ISBN 92-64-12017-3, 76 pp. .... US$ 6.00   £2.70   F24,00   DM12.00   Can. $ 7.20

TO BE PUBLISHED

UNITED STATES. FEDERAL POLICIES FOR EDUCATION FOR THE DISADVANTAGED

THE OECD CATALOGUE OF PUBLICATIONS and supplements will be sent free of charge on request addressed either to
OECD Publications Office, 2, rue André-Pascal, 75775 PARIS CEDEX 16,
or to the OECD Sales Agent in your country.

OECD SALES AGENTS
DÉPOSITAIRES DES PUBLICATIONS DE L'OCDE

ARGENTINA – ARGENTINE
Carlos Hirsch S.R.L., Florida 165, 4° Piso (Galería Guemes)
1333 BUENOS AIRES, Tel. 33.1787.2391 y 30.7122

AUSTRALIA – AUSTRALIE
Australia and New Zealand Book Company Pty. Ltd.,
10 Aquatic Drive, French Forest 2086 (P.O.B. 450)
BROOKVALE, 2100. Tel. 452.4411

AUSTRIA – AUTRICHE
OECD Publications and Information Center
4 Simrockstrasse 5300 BONN. Tel. (0228) 21.60.45
Local Agent/Agent local :
Gerold and Co., Graben 31, WIEN 1. Tel. 52.22.35

BELGIUM – BELGIQUE
LCLS
35, avenue de Stalingrad, 1000 BRUXELLES. Tel. 02.512.89.74

BRAZIL – BRÉSIL
Mestre Jou S.A., Rua Guaipa 518,
Caixa Postal 24090, 05089 SAO PAULO 10. Tel. 261.1920
Rua Senador Dantas 19 s/205-6, RIO DE JANEIRO GB.
Tel. 232.07.32

CANADA
Renouf Publishing Company Limited,
2182 St. Catherine Street West,
MONTRÉAL, Quebec H3H 1M7. Tel. (514)937.3519
522 West Hasting,
VANCOUVER, B.C. V6B 1L6. Tel. (604) 687.3320

DENMARK – DANEMARK
Munksgaard Export and Subscription Service
35, Nørre Søgade
DK 1370 KØBENHAVN K. Tel. +45.1.12.85.70

FINLAND – FINLANDE
Akateeminen Kirjakauppa
Keskuskatu 1, 00100 HELSINKI 10. Tel. 65.11.22

FRANCE
Bureau des Publications de l'OCDE,
2 rue André-Pascal, 75775 PARIS CEDEX 16. Tel. (1) 524.81.67
Principal correspondant :
13602 AIX-EN-PROVENCE : Librairie de l'Université.
Tel. 26.18.08

GERMANY – ALLEMAGNE
OECD Publications and Information Center
4 Simrockstrasse 5300 BONN. Tel. (0228) 21.60.45

GREECE – GRÈCE
Librairie Kauffmann, 28 rue du Stade,
ATHÈNES 132. Tel. 322.21.60

HONG-KONG
Government Information Services,
Sales and Publications Office, Baskerville House, 2nd floor,
13 Duddell Street, Central. Tel. 5.214375

ICELAND – ISLANDE
Snaebjörn Jönsson and Co., h.f.,
Hafnarstraeti 4 and 9, P.O.B. 1131, REYKJAVIK.
Tel. 13133/14281/11936

INDIA – INDE
Oxford Book and Stationery Co. :
NEW DELHI, Scindia House. Tel. 45896
CALCUTTA, 17 Park Street. Tel. 240832

INDONESIA – INDONÉSIE
PDIN-LIPI, P.O. Box 3065/JKT., JAKARTA, Tel. 583467

IRELAND – IRLANDE
TDC Publishers – Library Suppliers
12 North Frederick Street, DUBLIN 1 Tel. 744835-749677

ITALY – ITALIE
Libreria Commissionaria Sansoni :
Via Lamarmora 45, 50121 FIRENZE. Tel. 579751
Via Bartolini 29, 20155 MILANO. Tel. 365083
Sub-depositari :
Editrice e Libreria Herder,
Piazza Montecitorio 120, 00 186 ROMA. Tel. 6794628
Libreria Hoepli, Via Hoepli 5, 20121 MILANO. Tel. 865446
Libreria Lattes, Via Garibaldi 3, 10122 TORINO. Tel. 519274
La diffusione delle edizioni OCSE è inoltre assicurata dalle migliori librerie nelle città più importanti.

JAPAN – JAPON
OECD Publications and Information Center,
Landic Akasaka Bldg., 2-3-4 Akasaka,
Minato-ku, TOKYO 107 Tel. 586.2016

KOREA – CORÉE
Pan Korea Book Corporation,
P.O. Box n° 101 Kwangwhamun, SÉOUL. Tel. 72.7369

LEBANON – LIBAN
Documenta Scientifica/Redico,
Edison Building, Bliss Street, P.O. Box 5641, BEIRUT.
Tel. 354429 – 344425

MALAYSIA – MALAISIE
and/et SINGAPORE - SINGAPOUR
University of Malaysia Co-operative Bookshop Ltd.
P.O. Box 1127, Jalan Pantai Baru
KUALA LUMPUR. Tel. 51425, 54058, 54361

THE NETHERLANDS – PAYS-BAS
Staatsuitgeverij
Verzendboekhandel Chr. Plantijnstraat
S-GRAVENAGE. Tel. nr. 070.789911
Voor bestellingen: Tel. 070.789208

NEW ZEALAND – NOUVELLE-ZÉLANDE
Publications Section,
Government Printing Office,
WELLINGTON: Walter Street. Tel. 847.679
Mulgrave Street, Private Bag. Tel. 737.320
World Trade Building, Cubacade, Cuba Street. Tel. 849.572
AUCKLAND: Hannaford Burton Building,
Rutland Street, Private Bag. Tel. 32.919
CHRISTCHURCH: 159 Hereford Street, Private Bag. Tel. 797.142
HAMILTON: Alexandra Street, P.O. Box 857. Tel. 80.103
DUNEDIN: T & G Building, Princes Street, P.O. Box 1104.
Tel. 778.294

NORWAY – NORVÈGE
J.G. TANUM A/S Karl Johansgate 43
P.O. Box 1177 Sentrum OSLO 1. Tel. (02) 80.12.60

PAKISTAN
Mirza Book Agency, 65 Shahrah Quaid-E-Azam, LAHORE 3.
Tel. 66839

PHILIPPINES
National Book Store, Inc.
Library Services Division, P.O. Box 1934, MANILA.
Tel. Nos. 49.43.06 to 09, 40.53.45, 49.45.12

PORTUGAL
Livraria Portugal, Rua do Carmo 70-74,
1117 LISBOA CODEX. Tel. 360582/3

SPAIN – ESPAGNE
Mundi-Prensa Libros, S.A.
Castello 37, Apartado 1223, MADRID-1. Tel. 275.46.55
Libreria Bastinos, Pelayo 52, BARCELONA 1. Tel. 222.06.00

SWEDEN – SUÈDE
AB CE Fritzes Kungl Hovbokhandel,
Box 16 356, S 103 27 STH, Regeringsgatan 12,
DS STOCKHOLM. Tel. 08/23.89.00

SWITZERLAND – SUISSE
OECD Publications and Information Center
4 Simrockstrasse 5300 BONN. Tel. (0228) 21.60.45
Local Agents/Agents locaux
Librairie Payot, 6 rue Grenus, 1211 GENÈVE 11. Tel. 022.31.89.50
Freihofer A.G., Weinbergstr. 109, CH-8006 ZÜRICH.
Tel. 01.3624282

TAIWAN – FORMOSE
National Book Company,
84-5 Sing Sung South Rd, Sec. 3, TAIPEI 107. Tel. 321.0698

THAILAND – THAILANDE
Suksit Siam Co., Ltd., 1715 Rama IV Rd,
Samyan, BANGKOK 5. Tel. 2511630

UNITED KINGDOM – ROYAUME-UNI
H.M. Stationery Office, P.O.B. 569,
LONDON SE1 9NH. Tel. 01.928.6977, Ext. 410 or
49 High Holborn, LONDON WC1V 6 HB (personal callers)
Branches at: EDINBURGH, BIRMINGHAM, BRISTOL,
MANCHESTER, CARDIFF, BELFAST.

UNITED STATES OF AMERICA – ÉTATS-UNIS
OECD Publications and Information Center, Suite 1207,
1750 Pennsylvania Ave., N.W. WASHINGTON D.C.20006.
Tel. (202) 724.1857

VENEZUELA
Libreria del Este, Avda. F. Miranda 52, Edificio Galipan,
CARACAS 106. Tel. 32.23.01/33.26.04/33.24.73

YUGOSLAVIA – YOUGOSLAVIE
Jugoslovenska Knjiga, Terazije 27, P.O.B. 36, BEOGRAD.
Tel. 621.992

Les commandes provenant de pays où l'OCDE n'a pas encore désigné de dépositaire peuvent être adressées à :
OCDE, Bureau des Publications, 2, rue André-Pascal, 75775 PARIS CEDEX 16.
Orders and inquiries from countries where sales agents have not yet been appointed may be sent to:
OECD, Publications Office, 2 rue André-Pascal, 75775 PARIS CEDEX 16.

OECD PUBLICATIONS, 2, rue André-Pascal, 75775 PARIS CEDEX 16 - No. 41 723 1981
PRINTED IN FRANCE
(800 TD 91 81 03 1) ISBN 92-64-12150-1